278 FISHES IN FULL COLOR

FISHES

A GUIDE TO FRESH- AND SALT-WATER SPECIES

by
HERBERT S. ZIM, Ph.D.
and
HURST H. SHOEMAKER, Ph.D.
Associate Professor of Zoology Emeritus
University of Illinois

Illustrated by
JAMES GORDON IRVING

Atlantic Cutlassfish

D0465784

GOLDEN PRESS • NEW YORK
Western Publishing Company, Inc.
Racine, Wisconsin

FOREWORD

Golden Trout

Queen Triggerfish

Fishes have lived on the earth longer than any other backboned animals and show greater diversity in their way of life. If interest in fishes can be judged by interest in fishing, they are the most popular animals, too. With this book, the Golden Guides now encompass all the vertebrates—fishes, amphibians, reptiles, birds, and mammals.

Like previous Guides, the making of this book was a cooperative effort of authors, experts, artists, and publishers. We wish to thank the following organizations for the assistance they have given: University of Illinois Museum of Natural History; U.S. Fish and Wildlife Service; Gulf Coast Research Laboratory; The U.S. National Museum; Scripps Institution of Oceanography; Illinois Natural History Survey; and the Chicago Natural History Museum. Individual help from experts has been bountiful. May we especially thank Reeve M. Bailey, Frederick M. Bayer, Harvey R. Bullis, Jr., John E. Fitch, John R. Greeley, Gordon Gunter, Donald F. Hoffmeister, Carl L. Hubbs, R. Weldon Larimore, George G. Lower, Lawrence Page, Waldo L. Schmitt, Leonard P. Schultz, Henry F. Shirtz, Stewart Springer, Thomas Uzzell, Loren P. Woods, and Milton W. Zim.

H.S.Z.
H.H.S.

Revised Edition, 1987

This book is an introduction to the world of fishes—an important part of the greater world of aquatic life. It is primarily a guide to fishes as living animals and hence attempts to include most of the common fresh- and salt-water fishes of North American waters.

One problem in learning about fishes is that they are not easily seen except at an aquarium, or when caught. So, be prepared to identify fishes by using this book beforehand. Familiarity with fishes gained by thumbing through pages at odd moments may enable you to make rough identifications at sight. Use this book as an "arm-chair" guide, but also take it into the field with you, for that is where it can be used best. On fishing trips take it along in a plastic bag.

Use the table on the next two pages to help place in its proper group the fish you wish to identify. Then look through the proper section of the book for a picture of the fish, or one like it. Remember that only the more common species are illustrated. Their scientific names are on pp. 154-157. With these are abbreviations indicating where the fishes are found. Such notations refer to the species illustrated, not necessarily to the entire genus or family.

As a further help on ocean life, use SEASHORES, another Golden Guide. The book list on p. 153 introduces more advanced books. In using these, you may find it advantageous to know the scientific names of fishes.

3

The main groups of fishes

SHARKS and RAYS Have five or more gill openings, scales placoid, thornlike, or absent (terms are given on p. 12) **20-29**

STURGEONS and GARS Tail shark-like or rounded; ganoid scales **32-33**

HERRING-LIKE FISHES Fins without spines, pelvic fins on abdomen, tail forked, no adipose fin **34-41**

TROUTS, SALMONS Fins without spines; adipose fin, no barbels **42-50**

EELS, MINNOWS, SUCKERS, and CAT-FISHES Fins usually without spines, air bladder connected by a duct with alimentary canal **52-66**

FLYINGFISHES and relatives One or both of the jaws are elongate or the fishes have winglike fins **67-69**

COD-LIKE FISHES Usually three dorsal fins without spines **70-75**

FLATFISHES Lie on one side and have both eyes on upper side of head **76-78**

SEAHORSES and relatives Small mouth at end of long snout **80**

MULLETS, SILVERSIDES, and BARRACU-DAS Spiny dorsal fin, ventral fins located on the abdomen **81-83**

MACKERELS AND TUNAS Characterized by numerous finlets above and below the tail **84-89**

and their places in this book:

Brook Trout
cold fresh water

Channel Catfish
warm fresh water

Cod
cold salt water

Tarpon
warm salt water

**Eel—hatched in salt
water, lives in fresh**

Salmon — hatched in fresh water, lives in salt

STUDYING FISHES

FISHES, say dictionaries, are finned, backboned animals that live in water and breathe by means of gills. Modern fishes form a diverse, important, and challenging group of animals, not very well known in spite of the tremendous importance of commercial and recreational fishing. In this Guide we generally follow the scientific practice of using the plural form "fishes" to imply diversity of kinds, and the plural form "fish" in a more quantitative sense.

KINDS AND DISTRIBUTION

Experts estimate that there are about 30,000 species of fishes. Some species have world-wide distribution; some are limited to a single lake or stream. About 4,000 species are listed for North American waters. Florida records about 100 fresh- and 600 salt-water fishes; southern California, about 400. Many fishes live only in fresh water; many are marine; and a few divide their lives in between. Some prefer brackish water, where rivers mingle with the ocean. Some species live only in cold water; others in warm.

NAMES OF FISHES are often confusing. Both the popular names and the scientific names (pp. 154-157) used in this book follow A LIST OF COMMON AND SCIENTIFIC NAMES OF FISHES and its supplements, prepared by the American Fisheries Society. Wider use of these preferred names, which stress proper family relationships, will tend to reduce misunderstandings about names of fishes.

ADAPTATIONS of fishes are as intriguing as the fishes themselves. Swimming is characteristic of all fishes. Searobins and a few others can also crawl along the bottom with the aid of unusual fins. A number of fishes burrow in sand or mud; flyingfishes glide considerable distances in the air; eels migrate through wet grass; and Climbing Perch creep from pond to pond across the mud.

Fishes do not see very well, partly because of their eye structure and partly because, as one goes deeper in water, the light grows dimmer. Below 1,500 ft. fishes live in darkness. Fishes have, however, a well-developed sense of balance and of taste. Some have an excellent sense of touch also, this being aided by sensitive feelers (barbels) near the mouth. Fishes can hear; they are sensitive to vibrations, currents, and changes in temperature and pressure. Low-frequency vibrations are detected by organs in the lateral lines at their sides.

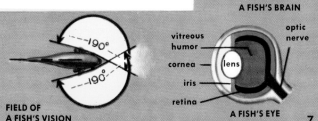

cerebellum   optic lobes   cerebral hemispheres

A FISH'S BRAIN

FIELD OF A FISH'S VISION

190°

190°

vitreous humor
cornea
iris
retina
lens
optic nerve

A FISH'S EYE

7

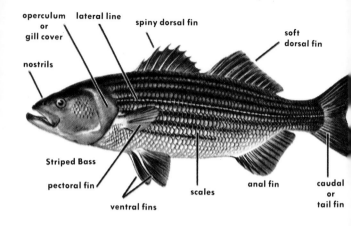

operculum or gill cover | lateral line | spiny dorsal fin | soft dorsal fin | nostrils | Striped Bass | pectoral fin | ventral fins | scales | anal fin | caudal or tail fin

PARTS OF FISHES

PARTS OF FISHES have distinct, precise names. Use them in identifying a fish. The fish pictured above is a typical bony fish (sharks, pp. 20-28, are somewhat different). Fishes have two sets of paired fins, the pectoral and the pelvic or ventral, corresponding to our arms and legs. They also have three unpaired fins: the dorsal or back; the caudal, or tail; and the anal. These differ in size and shape from fish to fish. An operculum covers the gills except in the shark and its relatives. Nostrils usually have two openings on each side. More highly developed fishes have a urogenital-tract opening separate from the anus. The ears have no external openings.

The scales (p. 12) on most bony fishes are often important in identification, because the number of rows of scales is constant for a species. The fins, used for balance and movement, are important, too. Their rays may be spiny or soft and branched. The dorsal fin often has two parts: the first, spiny, and the second, soft. The number of rays or spines in a fin counts in identification.

INTERNAL STRUCTURES of fishes set the pattern for all vertebrates. Bony fishes usually have four pairs of gills. Water passes through the mouth and over the gills, giving up some of the oxygen dissolved in it. The swim bladders of some fishes help in breathing. A two-chambered heart and a simple system of veins and arteries circulate the blood, which carries oxygen and digested food. Fishes usually have large mouths and teeth suited for grasping, tearing, or grinding. Food passes through a digestive tube and, with the aid of accessory glands, is converted into soluble form in the stomach and intestines. Digestive wastes are eliminated through the anus, and kidneys extract urine from the blood.

The head of fishes contains a brain simpler than, yet similar to, brains of other vertebrates. From it a spinal cord travels the length of the body, protected by the backbone. The skeleton of fishes is complex, with many small bones (as any diner on fish well knows). The eggs of the female and the sperm or milt of the male are usually discharged into the water, where the eggs are fertilized and the young develop.

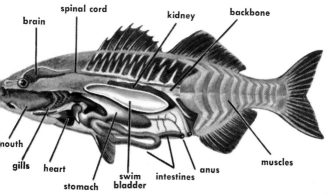

PELAGIC FISHES
(those that can live and feed well above the bottom)

Barracuda (1)
Halfbeak (2)
Mackerel (3)
Flyingfish
Tuna
Jacks
Dolphin
Harvestfish

BOTTOM FISHES
(those that live and feed at or near the bottom)

Stingray (1)
Bonefish (2)
Catfish (3)
Searobin
Flounder
Batfish
Spiny Dogfish
Paddlefish

FISH AND WATER are inseparable. The relationship is quite complex, for conditions of the water go far in determining the fish population. Some physical factors that affect fishes are temperature, depth (pressure), salinity, turbidity (undissolved solids), and the amount of dissolved oxygen. More oxygen, for example, dissolves in cold water than in warm water, and hence fishes such as trout, which need much oxygen, require colder water.

MIGRATIONS are common. Commercial and sport fishermen often depend on these movements to get bigger catches. Migrations may be from fresh to salt water or vice versa, toward or away from the surface, or north and south. Data on fish migrations are needed badly; anyone who finds a tagged fish should report it to the proper authorities.

Mackerel

Eel

Puffer

SHAPES of fishes usually have the streamlined pattern which is so efficient in the water. Mammals such as whales and dolphins that have returned to life in the seas have developed a similar form. Man uses streamlining in ships and submarines. Members of the mackerel family offer the best examples of streamlined fish form.

Fishes show a great range of departures from the streamlined shape. These many departures range all the way from the thin, almost ropelike eels to the triangular cowfish and the very flattened flounders. Each of these represents an adaptation to a specific way of life which puts a premium on something other than fast swimming. Flounders, for example, lie neatly camouflaged on the bottom, awaiting shrimp, other crustaceans, and small fishes on which they feed.

Dogfish

Butterfish

Pipefish

Flounder

11

placoid scales

ganoid scales

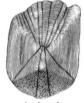

cycloid scales

ctenoid scales

SCALES AND TAILS Fishes are scaleless when hatched, but most develop scales the first year. Some fishes have rough scales with comblike edges (ctenoid scales); others have smooth (cycloid) scales. Scales of primitive fishes are heavy and platelike (ganoid); those of sharks are toothlike (placoid). Scales grow from pockets in the skin, growth being marked by rings. In winter, growth is usually less and rings are closer together, forming an annulus or annual ring. The number of these rings tells the age of a fish.

Tails reflect changes that have taken place through the ages. In sharks, as in early fossil fishes, the upper part of the tail, containing the backbone, extends to a point. In modern bony fishes, the tail is more balanced and the backbone ends where the tail begins.

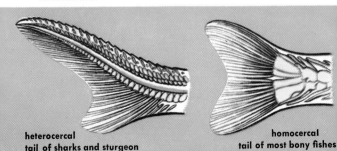

heterocercal
tail of sharks and sturgeon

homocercal
tail of most bony fishes

FISHING will long remain an important industry, for fish are among the least exploited of all the animals of direct use to man. About 83 million tons of fish are taken annually, and this harvest could be greatly increased. Nearly 98% of the fish harvest is taken in the northern hemisphere, about equally divided between the Atlantic and the Pacific. Some 50 species provide the bulk of commercial catches. Many other fishes that are edible or otherwise useful are not taken. In the United States alone, fisheries represent a 46-billion-dollar industry.

The oceans, which cover nearly three-quarters of the globe, contain far more plant life than is found on land. These limitless miles of "pasture"—mainly microscopic plants (phytoplankton)—support many millions of minute animals (zooplankton) which, in turn, are food for fishes.

FISHES AS WILDLIFE play an important part in the natural environment. Oceans, lakes, and rivers have their own natural communities of plant and animal life that include fishes. Fishes serve as food for many vertebrates. Shore and ocean birds probably consume much more than man. Fishes as wildlife furnish unparalleled sport for millions. No other sport has so many participants.

CONSERVATION is of growing importance to the world's fishes, even though they are so plentiful in numbers. The main peril to fishes is not the fisherman and his catch but the wastes of cities and industries, and results of poor farming. Water pollution, by sewage and industrial wastes, is a big problem in inland waters and in some bays and harbors. It may soon prove a threat to the oceans themselves. The increased erosion on farmland has silted and muddied nearby streams, destroying the fish in them. If you are interested in fishes, conservation—the wise use of all our natural resources—is your problem, too.

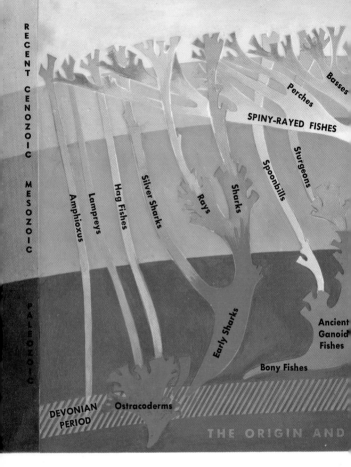

RECENT
CENOZOIC
MESOZOIC
PALEOZOIC

Basses
Perches
SPINY-RAYED FISHES
Sturgeons
Spoonbills
Sharks
Rays
Silver Sharks
Hag Fishes
Lampreys
Amphioxus

Early Sharks

Ancient
Ganoid
Fishes

Bony Fishes

DEVONIAN
PERIOD   Ostracoderms

THE ORIGIN AND

FISHES—the oldest major group of vertebrates—go back nearly a half-billion years. Fossilized fish bones and scales have been found in rocks 400 million years old. The Devonian period (about 350 million years ago) has been called the Age of Fishes because of the plentiful

14

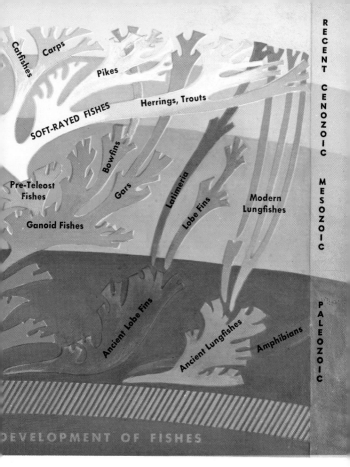

DEVELOPMENT OF FISHES

fish remains found in rocks of both oceanic and fresh-water origin. Some fishes have survived till today with scarcely a change. Many others have become extinct. Still others have given rise to new groups. The chart shows the family tree and evolution of fishes.

There is much that you can do with fishes besides fishing, and even this leading sport is enhanced by a knowledge of fishes and their habits. Research conducted by universities, by museums, and by government agencies continually reveals new and important facts about fishes. You too can contribute to this field of knowledge.

FIELD STUDIES   Any trained observer can contribute to our knowledge about fishes. Life histories of many species are still unknown. Much can still be learned about the behavior of common, easily observed species, but observations must be systematic and persistent to be worthwhile. Binoculars often help. Make a "water glass" or use a mask as a next step. Later you may want to go under water (with suitable equipment) for direct observation.

TANK STUDIES in aquaria may enable you to make observations that would otherwise be impossible. For fresh-water aquaria, use water from a pond, stream, or well. Add ample water plants, and do not overfeed the fish. Salt-water aquaria are more difficult. The water should be circulated and aerated by pumping. First, try only a few fishes in a large tank; then add eelgrass or other plants, and a few invertebrates. Several trials may be needed.

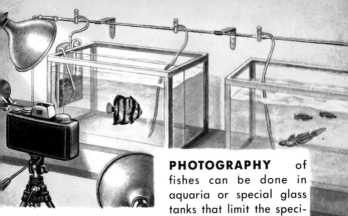

PHOTOGRAPHY of fishes can be done in aquaria or special glass tanks that limit the specimen's movements. Photography is rich and rewarding, especially with small, brightly colored fishes of warmer waters. The use of color, with the newer, faster films, can add much to your pictures of fishes. Flash or photoflood lighting is necessary indoors. Keep your eyes open for telling details.

SKIN DIVING opens new vistas for studying fishes in their natural environment. Surface and underwater observing can be as thrilling as hunting. But take time to develop the necessary skill; learn to work safely and unhurriedly to get the best results.

COLLECTING for scientific study is something quite different from fishing for sport or food. Making a collection of fishes is not as easy as collecting shells or flowers. The mounting of large specimens for exhibit calls for a skilled taxidermist. Smaller specimens for study can be preserved in alcohol (rubbing alcohol will do), but it is desirable first to fix them in a 10% solution of formalin. Inject preserving fluid into the body cavity of larger fish, or slit open the abdomen. Preserved fishes lose their color, but you can study other characteristics at leisure.

DETAILED IDENTIFICATION of fishes depends on characteristics which may look minor and unimportant to the uninitiated—structure of teeth, position and size of fins, shape of tail, type of scales, and the like. For such identification, actual possession of a fresh or preserved specimen is essential. So is experience in observing critical points and in using keys and reference books. First become familiar with the anatomy of fishes (pp. 8-9). Then, starting with fishes you know, use the keys found in the books listed on p. 153 until you feel sure of your methods. Finally try fishes with which you are not familiar.

SPECIAL STUDIES of fishes bring you to the border of scientific research. A good deal has been and can be done by amateurs. First, use this book to learn to identify common fishes. Then make a more systematic study of the fishes of your region. Begin to observe how fishes live, and by that time you will discover there is much of interest and importance which is not yet in books. From this to research is but a short step.

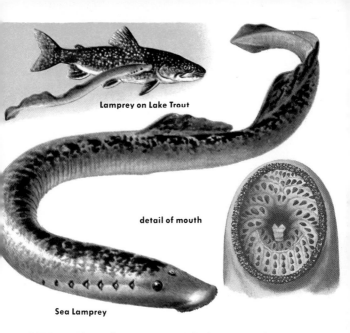

Lamprey on Lake Trout

detail of mouth

Sea Lamprey

LAMPREYS and HAGFISHES belong to a class separate from true fishes. Both lack jaws, but use their sucking mouths and rasping tongues to eat into the flesh of fish they attack. Lampreys, now a menace in the Great Lakes, spawn in tributary streams, laying their eggs in a shallow nest. Burrowing young remain in the streams about 3 years before returning to lakes or the sea. Some species grow 2 to 3 ft. long. Hagfishes or Slime Eels, blind and slimy, are common marine pests and scavengers in water over 100 ft. deep. They eat dead fish and those trapped in nets.

Atlantic Hagfish

19

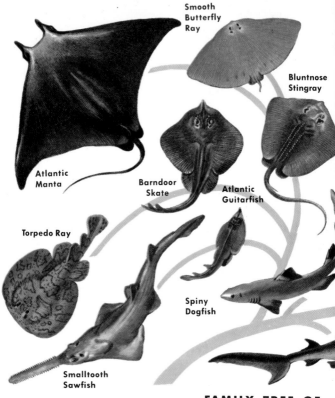

Smooth
Butterfly
Ray

Bluntnose
Stingray

Atlantic
Manta

Barndoor
Skate

Atlantic
Guitarfish

Torpedo Ray

Spiny
Dogfish

Smalltooth
Sawfish

FAMILY TREE OF

SHARKS and RAYS comprise one of the two groups of
true fishes. The other is the bony fishes. Sharks and rays
are primitive; some of them have changed little in 100
million years. Sharks and rays have no bones; their skel-

Spiny Dogfish Teeth

upper

lower

White Shark Teeth

side

front

Thresher

upper

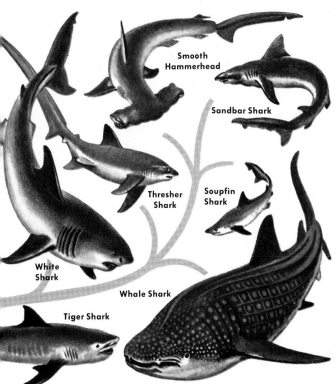

Smooth
Hammerhead

Sandbar Shark

Thresher
Shark

Soupfin
Shark

White
Shark

Whale Shark

Tiger Shark

SHARKS AND RAYS

etons are of cartilage, hardened by lime. They have small, toothlike (placoid) scales, and gills covered by several parallel slits. Of about 150 North American species, all are marine; a few invade fresh water.

Shark Teeth **Hammerhead Shark Teeth** **Tiger Shark Teeth**

lower

upper

lower

lower

upper

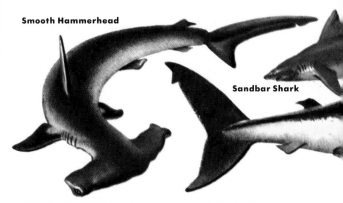

Smooth Hammerhead

Sandbar Shark

SMOOTH HAMMERHEAD has eyes at the ends of flattened extensions of its skull. This warm-water shark grows over 12 ft. long, may weigh over 1,000 lb. It lives near the surface, feeding on other fishes.

SPINY DOGFISH, a common pest of fishermen, grows to 4 ft. As in other sharks, female is larger than male. Eggs develop inside female; 2 to 11 young are born alive. Found in Atlantic and Pacific.

SANDBAR SHARK, common, grows to about 8 ft. Related to Tiger and Blue Sharks, both reputed "man-eaters." Found from the tropics north to New England, east into the Mediterranean. Feeds on bottom fishes.

NURSE SHARK is a large (6 to 10 ft.), sluggish shark of warm waters. A lazy scavenger, it is often found in shallows along Florida shores. It has a short, blunt head; small teeth and eyes.

Spiny Dogfish

Nurse Shark

White Shark

TIGER SHARK, 14 ft. or more, streamlined, prefers warm surface waters. Feeds on all kinds of sea life, including other sharks and rays. Notched saw-teeth, similar in both jaws. Young born alive; browner than adults; spotted.

WHITE SHARK, a tropical man-eater, grows well over 30 ft. Most often seen offshore. It feeds on seals and many kinds of fishes. Young are born alive. There is little danger from sharks in temperate coastal waters.

THRESHER SHARK, an unusual shark, has a long tail which it threshes back and forth in schools of small fish when feeding. Found in warm or temperate waters, the Thresher grows to 20 ft., over 1,000 lb. Shark is good eating; the Thresher especially so.

SOUPFIN SHARK is highly prized by Asians as food. It has been prized on the Pacific Coast, too, for its liver, rich in vitamin A. Possibly because of over-fishing, Soupfins are now rare. Grows about 6 ft. long; weight to 100 lb.

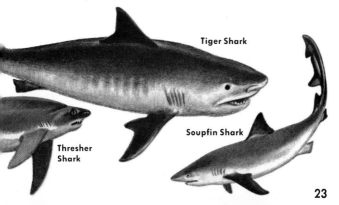

Tiger Shark

Soupfin Shark

Thresher Shark

23

WHALE SHARKS are the largest of all fishes. First discovered in 1828, they remained a mystery for some time. Now known in all warmer seas, Whale Sharks grow 45 ft. long, perhaps longer, and may weigh as much as 15 tons. A 38-ft. specimen captured near Florida showed the distinctive checkered and spotted pattern that marks Whale Sharks. These huge, harmless sharks swim close to the surface and feed by straining small sea animals out of the water much the same way as Baleen Whales. They have numerous, very small teeth in both jaws. Not much is known of the life history of these monsters. Young are hatched from eggs. Closely related to the Whale Shark is the slightly smaller Basking Shark, which has similar feeding habits. It lives in cooler waters and lacks the Whale Shark's markings. Neither shark is common.

ATLANTIC MANTA is the largest ray and the subject of some of the biggest fish fables. Despite its large size (it may be more than 20 ft. across and weigh well over a ton), it is not a dangerous fish, but feeds on crustaceans and small ocean life somewhat as the Whale Shark does. Its teeth are very small—perhaps useless. Most rays live at the bottom, but this one prefers the surface, often basking with its huge "wings" barely awash. Mantas, apparently in play, leap completely into the air, falling back into the water with a thundering slap. They are found widely in warmer waters and are common in the Gulf Stream. The flesh is good eating and is sometimes used as food. The harmless Manta is considered a sport fish in southern waters. It puts up a game fight when harpooned.

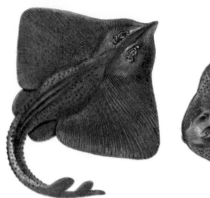

BARNDOOR SKATE, one of the largest (up to 5 ft. long), is generally found in water over 100 ft. deep along the Atlantic coast as far north as Nova Scotia. It has a pointed snout and a smooth skin. Food consists of bottom fish, crabs, and possibly shellfish. The egg case is large and greenish brown.

LITTLE SKATE, a fish of northern Atlantic waters, is found from the shore line down to depths of 300 ft. or more. Like all skates, it is a bottom feeder, living mainly on crustaceans. Identify it by its more rounded nose and the absence of spines on its back. Length to 20 in. "Wings" make good eating.

SKATES' EGG CASES may be found empty on almost every beach. Skates lay eggs, each in a horny container, nearly all year round. They hatch in 5 to 6 months, depending on water temperature. Egg cases vary in size from 1½ by 3 in. (exclusive of the horns) to over twice as big.

TORPEDO is a tropical ray. This squat, stubby fish has cells in its head which generate an electric current strong enough to give a severe shock. Usually under 3 ft. long—occasionally much larger. A similar species lives in the Pacific, and one other small electric ray occurs off Florida.

26

BLUNTNOSE STINGRAY and several similar species of large rays (Stingarees) found in warm waters have whiplike tails longer than their bodies, with a long stinger which can inflict painful wounds. These rays, of the Dasyatis group, may grow up to 7 ft. long. This stingray and its kin are diamond-shaped; they frequent shallow waters.

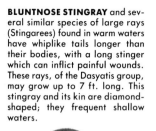

POISONOUS STINGERS (1 to 3 of them), located part way down the whiplike tail, mark most rays. They are sharply toothed, bony, and poisonous, causing painful wounds. If injured, squeeze wound and soak in hot water. Guard against infection. See a doctor unless healing is prompt.

SMOOTH BUTTERFLY RAY is a very broad ray with a very short tail and an almost triangular shape. The three species of Butterfly Rays all prefer warmer water, but are found as far north as Cape Cod on the Atlantic coast. Common in bays and other shallow areas; width up to 6 ft.

ROUND STINGRAYS are brown with scattered yellowish spots. These small rays (up to 24 in.) are common in shallow waters and are feared by swimmers because of their "stinger." Unlike skates, the young of rays are born alive. They bear from 2 to 8 young.

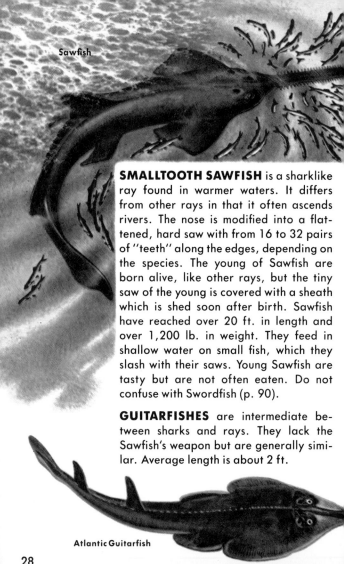

Sawfish

SMALLTOOTH SAWFISH is a sharklike ray found in warmer waters. It differs from other rays in that it often ascends rivers. The nose is modified into a flattened, hard saw with from 16 to 32 pairs of "teeth" along the edges, depending on the species. The young of Sawfish are born alive, like other rays, but the tiny saw of the young is covered with a sheath which is shed soon after birth. Sawfish have reached over 20 ft. in length and over 1,200 lb. in weight. They feed in shallow water on small fish, which they slash with their saws. Young Sawfish are tasty but are not often eaten. Do not confuse with Swordfish (p. 90).

GUITARFISHES are intermediate between sharks and rays. They lack the Sawfish's weapon but are generally similar. Average length is about 2 ft.

Atlantic Guitarfish

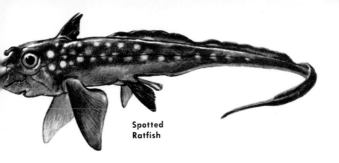

Spotted
Ratfish

CHIMAERAS and RATFISHES represent a small but interesting group of fishes intermediate between the sharks and bony fishes. Their skeletons are similar to those of sharks. They have only a single gill opening, like the bony fishes, but the gill cover is not bony. Chimaeras and Ratfishes are worldwide, mainly in deep water. The Atlantic Chimaeras are up to 3 ft. long. Ratfishes are found in the Gulf of Mexico and in the Pacific, where they range north to Alaska. One Pacific species enters shallow water. Ratfishes lay eggs in ridged capsules something like those of skates. The back spines are reportedly poisonous. Male Ratfishes and Chimaeras have a sharp-spined, clublike growth between the eyes and reproductive organs attached to the pelvic fins.

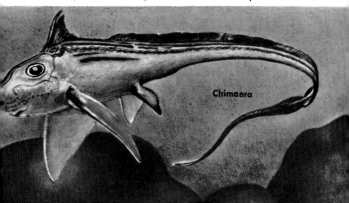

Chimaera

A FAMILY TREE OF BONY FISHES

THE BONY FISHES are the most recent, best known, and most widely distributed fishes. They form the largest class of backboned animals—about 30,000 species. Since they are so variable, common characteristics are hard to single out; some of these are given on the facing page.

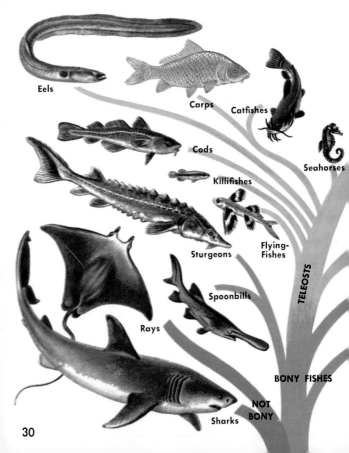

Eels

Carps

Catfishes

Cods

Seahorses

Killifishes

Sturgeons

Flying-Fishes

Spoonbills

TELEOSTS

Rays

BONY FISHES

NOT BONY

Sharks

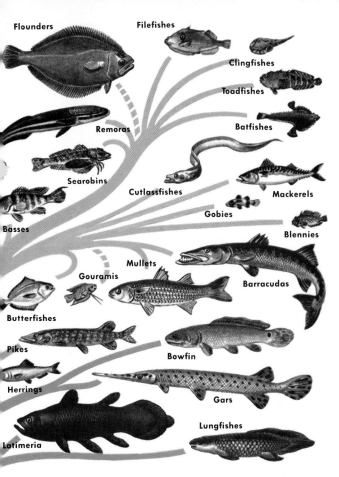

Flounders
Filefishes
Clingfishes
Toadfishes
Batfishes
Remoras
Searobins
Cutlassfishes
Mackerels
Gobies
Basses
Blennies
Mullets
Barracudas
Gouramis
Butterfishes
Pikes
Bowfin
Herrings
Gars
Latimeria
Lungfishes

Bony fishes may be flat, round, or distorted. Scales or fins may be reduced or absent. The single pair of gill openings has bony coverings. The largest fish is the Whale Shark; the smallest is a goby less than an inch long.

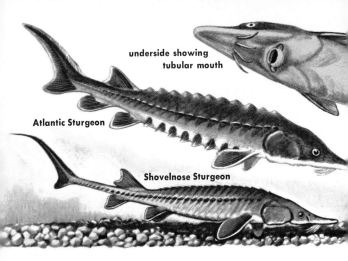

underside showing
tubular mouth

Atlantic Sturgeon

Shovelnose Sturgeon

STURGEONS   Atlantic Sturgeon resembles the famed
European species; the black eggs of the female make
fine caviar. These are fishes of ancient lineage (pp. 30-31),
with stiff bony plates and primitive tails. They swim along
the bottom with chin barbels just touching the sand. When
these sensitive feelers touch small animals, the sturgeon
shoots out its tubular mouth and sucks in its dinner. Other
North American sturgeons include smaller Lake Sturgeon
(2 ft.), Shovelnose Sturgeon, and White Sturgeon of the
West Coast. This and the Atlantic Sturgeon grow to over
10 ft. The Paddlefish, a fresh-water relative, has become
rare in recent years.

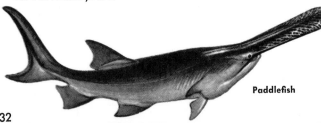

Paddlefish

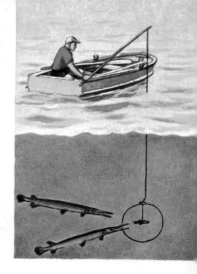

GARS, like sturgeons, are fishes of an American family which was widespread in ancient times. All prefer warm water, where they prey on other American fishes; they have a lung-like swim bladder that supplements the gills in the absorption of oxygen in summer when the supply in the water is low. Milt and roe of gars are poisonous (as is true of several other fishes). Gars are active, armored, and not easily caught. Sometimes "gar-rodeos" are held to capture gars by wire snares. The Shortnose Gar occurs less commonly in brackish water of bays than the Longnose, Spotted, and Alligator Gars. All inhabit fresh-water rivers and lakes of the Mississippi basin. The Alligator Gar (4 to 6 ft.) is the largest.

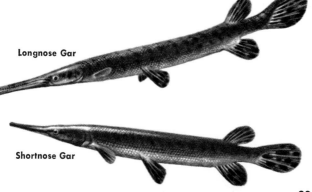

Longnose Gar

Shortnose Gar

TARPON, LADYFISH, and BONEFISH represent three species similar to the herrings (pp. 36-40). All are favorites of sportsmen, but once caught, these bony fishes are usually turned loose to fight again. And they are terrific fighters, as enthusiasts will testify.

Tarpon, famous for its spectacular leaps, is largest and best known, averaging about 4 ft. long and 60 lb., though occasionally much larger and heavier. Tarpon has a blue-gray back, shading into bright silver on the sides, with an occasional touch of yellow on the fins. It has a long, trailing dorsal fin; coarse scales, sometimes over an inch across; and a large mouth with minute teeth. Tarpon come into shallow water and up into rivers to feed on smaller fish. Found only in summer in the northern part of its range.

Ladyfish, sometimes known as Ten-Pounder, is smaller than Tarpon but like it has a bony plate under the throat. It, too, prefers bays, inlets, and mouths of rivers, and is valued more as game than as a food fish. Prefers warmer waters. A 10-lb. Ladyfish is large; 2 or 3 lb. is the more usual weight. Has a similar relative in the warmer waters of the Pacific.

Bonefish is the last of these silver-sided game fishes. This one also prefers shallow water in grass beds and inlets but does not ascend rivers. Bonefish have mouths

Ladyfish

34

Tarpon

that open downward, indicating bottom feeding. They live on crabs and mollusks, and are generally caught with live bait, such as shrimp. The sportsman may take hours to locate Bonefish and hours more to hook one before he enjoys the thrill of the fight.

Bonefish

Alewife

HERRING FAMILY includes fishes with compressed bodies tapering to a sharp keel. Fins are without spines, and the pelvic fins are on the abdomen. The tail is forked and there is no adipose fin. Herring are abundant, a prime food of predaceous fishes, and comprise more of the commercial catch than all other families combined.

ALEWIFE, a member of the herring family, similar to Shad, was once very common and is still of commercial importance. These prolific fish (sometimes called Branch Herring) live in coastal waters. They move up rivers to spawn in spring just before the Shad. Young remain in the rivers till fall. Then, 2 to 4 in. long, they swim back to sea, where they grow to about 10 to 12 in. (maximum, 15 in.) and to a weight of 1 lb. Alewife are caught in nets as they move upstream, and are sold as herring. They are used for oil and in feed products. The Hickory Shad, a more southern species, is similar, but has a more tapering head and a thicker body.

AMERICAN SHAD, aristocrat of the herrings, has a life history similar to the Alewife's. It too is netted as it ascends rivers to spawn. But it is a larger, more tasty fish, prized as a table delicacy. Shad average under 2 ft. long and about 4 lb. in weight, though they may grow more than twice as heavy. Shad was one of the first fishes to be artificially propagated. Introduced along the Pacific in 1870, Shad soon became a commercial fish. It was once abundant all along the Atlantic, but stream pollution has cut the catch to less than one-fifth of its past average. Now, under good management, Shad are returning to some of the eastern rivers.

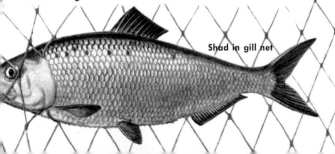

Shad in gill net

PACIFIC SARDINES, often called Pilchards or California Sardines, are most familiar in cans. Whatever their name, these members of the herring family are one of our important commercial fishes. Over half a million tons are caught annually, most of the catch going directly into canned fish and industrial products. Pacific Sardines are a fish of open seas, moving in great schools. Special sardine boats with giant purse seines haul in the catch. The young move closer to shore to feed on plankton. As they mature they move seaward again, and in one to three years grow 7 to 10 inches long. They may live as long as ten years.

Pacific Sardine young are prized as bait fish. The Pacific tuna boats use millions of pounds yearly as bait in tuna fishing.

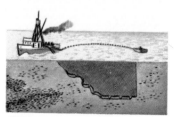

Setting purse seine over side of trawler. Skiff acts as a drag.

The purse seine sets around a school of sardines.

ATLANTIC MENHADEN or Mossbunker is an important commercial fish, though rarely used as food. Oil from them is used in chemical industries; Menhaden fish meal goes into many prepared foods for animals. Menhaden are open-water fish found all along the Atlantic. Though common, not much is known about them. Most are caught in the fall when large schools move southward, to return again the next spring. The schools swim close to the surface and are recognized at a distance by the gulls hovering above and feeding on them. Large numbers of young find their way into bays and inlets, where they feed and grow up to 5 or 6 in. the first year. In three years the Menhaden are mature. By that time they are 8 to 10 in. long and weigh ½ lb. They occasionally grow up to 18 in. The Gulf Menhaden is very similar.

he seine is shut and most of the et hauled aboard.

Fish are bailed out. Part of the seine remains in the water.

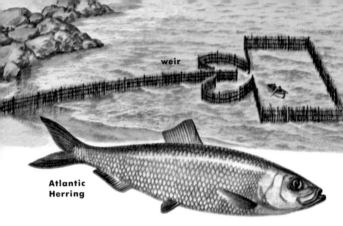

weir

Atlantic Herring

HERRING are more famous in Europe than in this country, yet are important food fish of our Atlantic and Pacific fisheries. The Atlantic and Pacific Herring are different subspecies, but quite similar in appearance and habits. Both live in large schools, feeding on plankton. In fall they move toward shore to spawn; females lay about 30,000 eggs each. The young stay near shore and, in New England, are caught in weirs at this period. Young Herring form the New England "sardine" catch. Herring mature in three years and are then about 10 in. long; they may grow up to 18 in. A number of other members of the herring family include the Gizzard Shad (with a tough, muscular stomach) and the Thread Herring, a more southern fish with a thread-like extension of its dorsal fin, like the Tarpon's.

Gizzard Shad

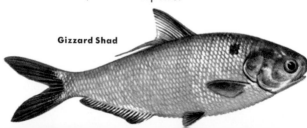

Bay Anchovy

ANCHOVIES are small fish, closely related to herring, common along both coasts. On the Atlantic, the commonest species rarely venture north of Cape Cod. Anchovies are caught the entire length of our Pacific shoreline, but are more plentiful to the south. Not very much is known about their habits, but the Pacific species is numerous and is a commercial fishing resource. Anchovies are gregarious, often traveling in large schools.

The characteristics of the family include abdominal pelvic fins and a single small dorsal fin. Anchovies lack scales on their heads and do not have a lateral line. The lower jaw is distinctive.

Bay Anchovy of the Atlantic (3 to 4 in. long) has a large, gaping mouth. Note its large scales and deeply forked tail.

Northern Anchovy

Northern Anchovy, a common and abundant Pacific species, is larger (up to 9 in.). It spawns throughout the year. One form lives in brackish water. Anchovies feed on copepods and other plankton. They are, in turn, food for many pelagic or open-sea fishes.

SALMON and trout form a family renowned as food and game fish. The Pacific salmon (at least six species) are best known, being the basis of a 38-million-dollar industry. Mature males differ from other salmon and trout in having both jaws hooked. All have a large number of rays (14 to 17) in the anal fin. Salmon have an extra fatty (adipose) fin on the back near the tail. Pacific salmon breed in rivers; young return to the sea to mature. The annual runs of breeding salmon at the mouths of streams climax a most unusual migration cycle.

Pink Salmon

Chum Salmon

CHINOOK or King Salmon is the largest salmon, reaching 100 lb. and averaging about 25. Found north from Monterey Bay, it migrates far up the larger rivers to breed, mainly in spring or fall. The Chinook, like others, varies in color with age, sex, and season.

CHUM or Dog Salmon, smaller than Chinook, has a longer head. It spawns closer to the mouths of rivers and so has not been too badly affected by dams. Length, about 18 in.; weight, 10 to 20 lb. Occurs north of Sacramento River to Alaska.

Chinook Salmon

Coho Salmon

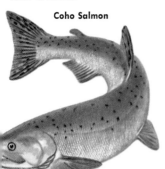

PINK or Humpback Salmon may be found farther south than others. Its migration is short; spawning is done within a few miles upstream. This pink-fleshed salmon is one of the smaller species (5 to 7 lb.). The male, before spawning, develops a hump on its back and twisted hooked jaws.

COHO or Silver Salmon is another smaller species (5 to 8 lb.) found from Monterey north, and common around Puget Sound. It does not spawn as far upstream as the Chinook. The silvery males become red in spawning season.

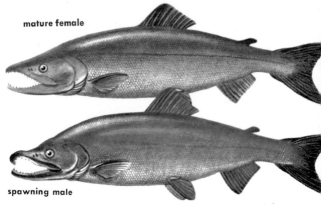

mature female

spawning male

egg

Alevin: just hatched; after 5 to 6 months

Alevin: yolk sac is absorbed in about 6 weeks

SOCKEYE or Red Salmon is prized for its deep red flesh of excellent flavor. Found north of Monterey, it is a smaller salmon, averaging 5 to 6 lb., occasionally twice that. It has been introduced into New England and has also become a landlocked species in a few lakes. The Sockeye illustrates the remarkable color change the male undergoes during the breeding season. The adults die after spawning far upstream. The fertilized eggs, after passing through various stages similar to those illustrated below, develop into fingerlings, which find their way to the sea.

DEVELOPMENT OF ATLANTIC SALMON

Parr: feeds and swims freely—about 2 years

Parr becomes smolt as it begins journey to the sea

Sebago Salmon

Atlantic Salmon

ATLANTIC SALMON, to some people, is *the* game fish. Once common in New England streams, it has retreated before dams and water pollution. Usually a good-sized fish (average 8 to 12 lb.), it may exceed 50 lb. After two to four years at sea, an Atlantic Salmon returns to the rivers to spawn, but does not necessarily die like the Pacific salmon. It spawns in fall, with eggs hatching the following spring. The Sebago Salmon is a smaller, land-locked form of the Atlantic Salmon; it spawns in the tributary streams of New England lakes.

CUTTHROAT TROUT varies in size and color. A gamy western fish, it sometimes migrates to sea. Averages 9 in.

TROUT, close relatives of salmon, generally prefer fresh water. Several species return to the sea, and then their appearance often changes, causing sportsmen endless confusion. The Brown Trout introduced from Europe does better in warmer waters than our native species (below). It is marked with large, light-bordered red spots; often weighs 5 lb. Our native trout require colder water, especially for spawning. They feed on insects, crustaceans, and smaller fish. Trout are often raised in hatcheries and released in suitable fishing waters.

RAINBOW TROUT is a western species with many local forms. Transferred widely to colder eastern streams and lakes, where it does well. "Steelheads" are Rainbows which go to sea. These large trout average 2 to 5 lb., may occasionally reach 40 lb.

DOLLY VARDEN is another western trout which may take to the sea. This one is a voracious feeder on young trout and so has a mixed reputation. Dolly Vardens are hardy and still plentiful. Like Brook Trout, they have light stripes on the lower fins.

BROOK TROUT is an eastern trout that has been introduced into western streams. It is smaller than the Dolly Varden but otherwise looks similar. Markings more mottled; fins have white edges. Weight about 2 lb., rarely up to 10. Thrives in water below 50°F.

LAKE TROUT are cold-water fish of larger, deep lakes in northern U.S. and Canada; a commercial food fish in the Great Lakes and a game fish everywhere. Prefer deep water in summer, shallow water in fall. They are the largest trout, average 6 lb.

McGinty   Royal Coachman   Chief Needabah   Bob Wilsc

TROUT FLIES

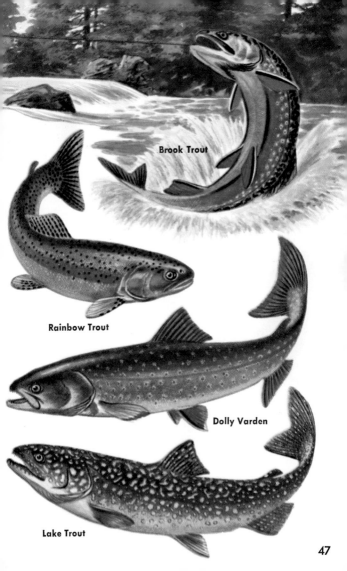

Brook Trout

Rainbow Trout

Dolly Varden

Lake Trout

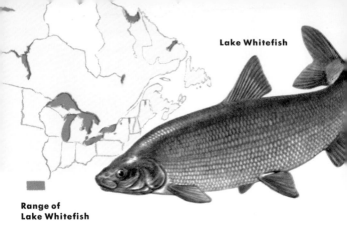

Lake Whitefish

Range of
Lake Whitefish

THE WHITEFISH FAMILY includes our most important inland food fishes of northern waters. They are related to the salmon but have larger scales and smaller mouths, with few or no teeth. Like salmon, they have an adipose fin near the tail. Most are lake fish. The various members of this family are not easy to distinguish without detailed study of nostrils, teeth, and gill rakers.

Lake Whitefish are fairly large, averaging 22 in. and 3½ lb.; a few have reached 20 lb. or more. The largest are in Lake Superior, but whitefish are found in all the Great Lakes and have been transplanted to other deep northern ones. Lake Whitefish feed on aquatic insects and crustaceans. They prefer deep water except when spawning in fall. The supply of these Whitefish is badly depleted and the species is threatened.

Shortjaw Cisco

Cisco

Round Whitefish

CISCO or **LAKE HERRING** is not a true herring but a whitefish. It lives in large schools near the surface, but often goes down a hundred feet or more. In early winter this Cisco comes close to shore to spawn. The female lays her eggs on the bottom in water 25 ft. deep or less. These Ciscos feed on plankton, small crustaceans, and insects. They grow to 12 in. long and, next to the Lake Whitefish, are considered the best lake species for eating or smoking.

ARCTIC GRAYLING, not in the whitefish family, is closely related. It is marked by a long, soft, dorsal fin. Although once common in the Great Lakes, it now thrives only in the upper Missouri valley.

SHORTJAW CISCOS are almost as important in commercial lake fishing as Shallow-water Ciscos, which they closely resemble. They too grow about 12 in. long and are abundant in deep waters (mainly about 180 ft.) of Lake Superior and other lakes. Food like that of the Lake Whitefish. Spawns in November.

ROUND WHITEFISH or Pilotfish is a close relative of the Lake Whitefish but differs from it in having a rounder cross section and a more deeply colored back. Its weight averages from 3 to 4 lb. Found in all the Great Lakes except Lake Erie, it ranges north through the Canadian lakes and in New England. These once-common fish have now become very scarce.

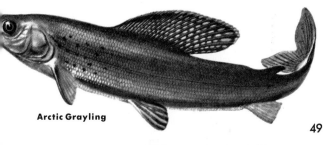

Arctic Grayling

49

A Smelt run

SMELTS show their relationship to salmon in the short adipose fin near the tail. However, they are much smaller, averaging 7-9 in. long (rarely over 1 ft.) and weighing about 6 oz. The American Smelt is a salt-water fish, living in a narrow belt close to shore. In spring it moves up rivers to spawn. Those that have been transplanted into the Great Lakes and others move into streams for spring spawning. At this time they are caught in great numbers with nets, dipnets, and hooks.

Rainbow Smelt

Whitebait Smelt, or Whitebait, is the best known of several Pacific smelts found in abundance in the waters north of San Francisco. The Candlefish, a very oily species, was once used by Indians as fuel. The Deep Sea Smelt or Argentine, of a related family, is a slightly larger fish with a smaller mouth.

Whitebait Smelt

Hatchetfish   Lanternfish

LANTERNFISH and about a dozen other small species representing half a dozen families all possess luminescent organs which make them shine in the dark. Most of these are fish of the open ocean, living at moderate depths— about 500 ft. They are sometimes responsible for the flashes of light one sees around and below ships at night. (But many other kinds of luminescent animals live in the sea besides these fish.) The Lanternfish is about 3 in. long; other species are twice the size. They are found in both the Atlantic and the Pacific. So are the small (up to 3 in.) Hatchetfish; these thin, large-eyed fish have oversized mouths and several rows of light organs. Other luminescent fishes include the Viperfish and the Midshipman (p. 141).

Hatchetfish and Lanternfish in the black depths.

EELS represent a large and unusual order of fishes, including 13 families and about 140 North American species. Common characteristics are their snakelike shape, lack of spines in the fins, and the absence of ventral fins. Gill openings are small; and the tiny scales when present are embedded in the skin and practically invisible.

American Eel

American Eel is at the same time one of the best known and one of the most mysterious of fishes. Its life history was practically unknown till the 20th century, and even now the story is far from complete. Both the European and the American Eel spawn in the same deep waters south of Bermuda. Mature adults come to this area from both sides of the Atlantic. The females are prolific; each lays about ten million eggs. The adults probably die after breeding. The larvae—small, flattened, and transparent—begin to move toward their

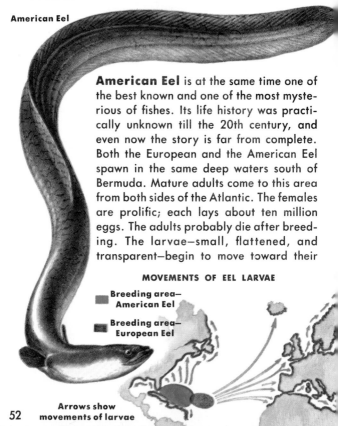

MOVEMENTS OF EEL LARVAE

■ Breeding area—
American Eel

■ Breeding area—
European Eel

52   Arrows show
movements of larvae

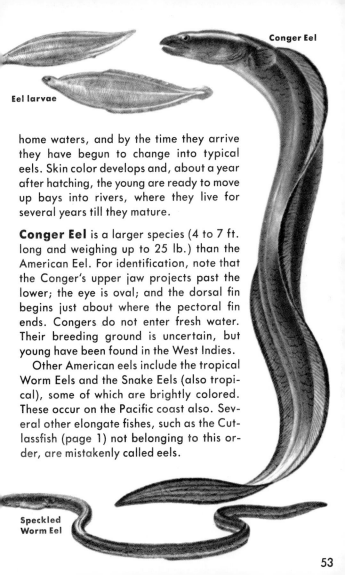

Conger Eel

Eel larvae

home waters, and by the time they arrive they have begun to change into typical eels. Skin color develops and, about a year after hatching, the young are ready to move up bays into rivers, where they live for several years till they mature.

Conger Eel is a larger species (4 to 7 ft. long and weighing up to 25 lb.) than the American Eel. For identification, note that the Conger's upper jaw projects past the lower; the eye is oval; and the dorsal fin begins just about where the pectoral fin ends. Congers do not enter fresh water. Their breeding ground is uncertain, but young have been found in the West Indies.

Other American eels include the tropical Worm Eels and the Snake Eels (also tropical), some of which are brightly colored. These occur on the Pacific coast also. Several other elongate fishes, such as the Cutlassfish (page 1) not belonging to this order, are mistakenly called eels.

Speckled Worm Eel

53

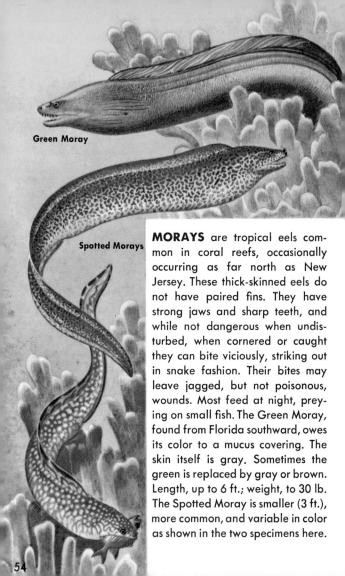

Green Moray

Spotted Morays

MORAYS are tropical eels common in coral reefs, occasionally occurring as far north as New Jersey. These thick-skinned eels do not have paired fins. They have strong jaws and sharp teeth, and while not dangerous when undisturbed, when cornered or caught they can bite viciously, striking out in snake fashion. Their bites may leave jagged, but not poisonous, wounds. Most feed at night, preying on small fish. The Green Moray, found from Florida southward, owes its color to a mucus covering. The skin itself is gray. Sometimes the green is replaced by gray or brown. Length, up to 6 ft.; weight, to 30 lb. The Spotted Moray is smaller (3 ft.), more common, and variable in color as shown in the two specimens here.

BUFFALOS introduce the sucker family, a group of fresh-water bottom feeders. Of about 100 kinds of suckers, many are food fish. Buffalos are large, coarse, and somewhat bony suckers, common in rivers and lakes all through the central states, where they rank highest among the commercial species. Look for them in quiet or sluggish water, where they feed on mollusks, aquatic insect larvae, and water plants. The Bigmouth Buffalo may grow up to 4 ft. long, weighing 65 lb., but is usually much smaller. It spawns from April to June in shallow water; eggs hatch in about 10 days. The mouth is directed forward rather than down, unlike the mouths in other buffalos. The Smallmouth Buffalo is a smaller fish rarely reaching 20 lb. The Black Buffalo is an intermediate species, as regards both position of mouth and depth of body.

top: Smallmouth Buffalo   bottom: Bigmouth Buffalo

OTHER SUCKERS are widespread in rivers and lakes of the Mississippi basin. Some are commercial food fish; some are so easily caught that every child knows them.

White Sucker

HOG SUCKER grows to 2 ft. but is usually smaller. Often seen grubbing through pebbles, with its snout protruded, probing for bottom life. Prefers clear, fast streams. Found from Alabama and Oklahoma northward to New York and Minnesota.

WHITE SUCKERS, though bony, are netted as food fish because of their firm, sweet flesh. They are variable in color; fins become red in spring and males become darker then, as these fish enter small creeks to spawn. Length: up to 20 in.

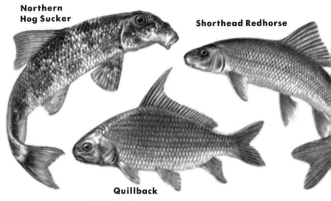

Northern Hog Sucker

Shorthead Redhorse

Quillback

QUILLBACK and River Carpsucker are both called American Carp, though neither is related to the carp (p. 57). Both are well-known native suckers, often netted in lakes and rivers. Quillbacks run to 5 or 6 lb.

SHORTHEAD REDHORSE is one of a group of suckers with reddish fins; the dorsal is short. It is one of the tastiest suckers, growing to 2 ft.; weighs 8 to 10 lb. Redhorses are coarse-scaled; prefer clear streams and lakes.

CARP are the largest minnows—a big family (p. 58) including over 300 American species, mainly small, freshwater fishes. The term "minnow" is loosely used for many small fishes. True minnows (family *Cyprinidae*) are soft-rayed fishes with teeth in the throat only. Carp were brought to Europe from Asia and from Europe to America in the 1870's and '80's. Widely transplanted, they are now found from coast to coast in lakes and slow streams. Carp are bottom feeders, often muddying the water so much that aquatic plants cannot grow. However, Carp are here to stay and have proved a valuable commercial fish. They are occasionally hooked, with doughballs as the favorite bait, but more often are netted. They grow up to 3 ft. long, weighing 20 lb. or more. Young grow rapidly. Most Carp are scaled, but Mirror Carp have only a few large scattered scales, and Leather Carp have no scales at all. The goldfish raised in aquaria and ponds are very similar to Carp and are of the same family.

REDSIDE DACE (4 in.) occurs in the northeast and in clear midwest creeks. Males in spring have crimson sides.

MINNOWS, other than Carp (p. 57), are mainly small fish, and while a few grow large enough to be used for food, most play a more indirect role as far as man is concerned. They are a favorite bait fish, and selling them is a sizable industry. More important in the long run is the natural role of minnows as consumers of aquatic insects and crustacea, and as food for larger, more valuable fish. Minnows, and similar small fishes, help maintain a plentiful supply of sport fish. They are an essential link in the cycle of fresh-water aquatic life.

CREEK CHUB is a large minnow (to 12 in.) with a black spot on the front of its dorsal fin. In spring, tubercules develop on the head. Found widely in small streams; occasionally in lakes. Male builds gravel nest for fertilized eggs. A good sports fish when trout are scarce.

GOLDEN SHINER is golden during the breeding season; otherwise the back is greenish and only the sides have a trace of gold. This hardy fish seems better able than others to survive in small ponds during winter, when the oxygen content of the water is low. Length: 5 in., rarely up to 12.

Thicktail Chub

Southern Redbelly Dace

THICKTAIL or **SACRAMENTO CHUB** is abundant in the rivers of the California Valley. It is one of a few members of the minnow family to be found in the Pacific drainage. Note the dark spots on the scales. Its color is usually a dull brown. Length: up to 12 in.

EMERALD SHINER, a very common species in lakes and clear streams, is named for its greenish back. The Emerald Shiner shows a preference for lakes. Large schools of young are often seen. Widely distributed through the Mississippi Valley and north into Canada.

REDBELLY DACES include a northern and a southern species with very similar markings. The parallel back stripes are characteristic. Males are brightly colored; bellies are scarlet in the spring, otherwise silvery. Length 3 to 4 in.

CUTLIPS MINNOW is most common in eastern streams and rivers. Named for the mouth and jaw structure, which can be seen only when the fish is turned over. It has a blackish bar behind the gill covers. Grows up to nearly 6 in. long.

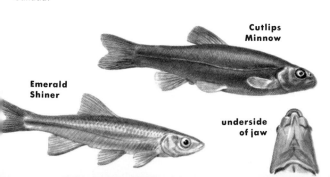

Cutlips Minnow

Emerald Shiner

underside of jaw

CATFISHES are best known as warm-water, fresh-water fishes. However, this large group (over 30 species) includes the bullheads (p. 62) and the Hardhead Catfish (p. 63). Catfishes rank second only to buffalos as fresh-water commercial fishes. If combined with bullheads they are first. European Catfish, 12 ft. long, have been reported. Catfishes take a wide variety of food, including clams, insect larvae, and crustaceans. They are also scavengers. Some live in muddy waters where other fishes do not live. Catfishes are taken on lines or in hoop nets as above.

Large-sized catfish are edible and tasty. All have smooth, scaleless bodies, long barbels around the mouth, and spines in the dorsal and pectoral fins which are irritating and perhaps poisonous. None is found in the Pacific Coast states except the White Catfish, introduced into California.

Channel Catfish, with deeply forked tail and fairly slender body, is probably best known. It prefers clear, moving water; can weigh up to 20 lb., usually 3 or 4.

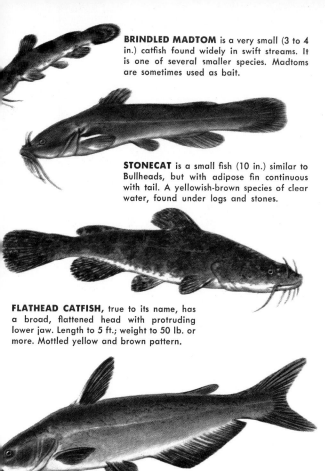

BRINDLED MADTOM is a very small (3 to 4 in.) catfish found widely in swift streams. It is one of several smaller species. Madtoms are sometimes used as bait.

STONECAT is a small fish (10 in.) similar to Bullheads, but with adipose fin continuous with tail. A yellowish-brown species of clear water, found under logs and stones.

FLATHEAD CATFISH, true to its name, has a broad, flattened head with protruding lower jaw. Length to 5 ft.; weight to 50 lb. or more. Mottled yellow and brown pattern.

BLUE CATFISH is the largest catfish in the Mississippi drainage; it can weigh over 150 lb. Note blue-gray back and silvery belly. Fine eating.

Black Bullhead

Yellow Bullhead

Brown Bullhead

BULLHEADS are small catfish which rarely grow over a foot long or weigh over 2 lb. They live in muddy ponds and streams and may survive in the mud when ponds "dry up." They feed on almost any kind of plant and animal life they find along the bottom. Much of their food is snails, crayfish, and insects. Bullheads are good eating, though the flesh may have a muddy flavor. They spawn in spring, making a nest on the hard bottom. The male watches the nest and guards the young. Bullheads have a square or slightly rounded tail, and are often mottled yellowish in color. Three species, common in central and eastern waters, are shown above.

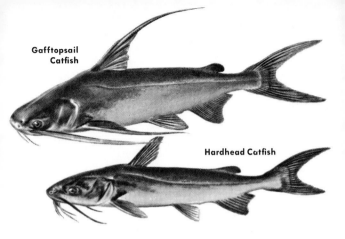

Gafftopsail
Catfish

Hardhead Catfish

MARINE CATFISHES are common in bays and harbors along the Atlantic and Gulf coasts in summer. They winter in deeper water. These southern species are usually found south of Virginia and the Carolinas, rarely north to Cape Cod. The Gafftopsail Catfish is named for its long, ribbonlike pectoral and dorsal fins. It has two barbels on the lower jaw. Length, to 2 ft.; weight, 3 to 4 lb. The Hardhead Catfish is smaller, and is considered a "trash" fish.

Both these catfish put an unusual burden on the male during breeding. The male carries the fertilized eggs in his mouth for about two months, going without food until well after they hatch, as the young continue to stay in this curious nest.

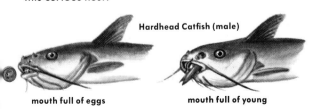

Hardhead Catfish (male)

mouth full of eggs   mouth full of young

PIKE, PICKEREL, and MUSKELLUNGE form a small but famous group of long, thin fishes. All have spineless dorsal fins and large anal fins; long, narrow jaws with sharp teeth. They eat small fishes and crayfish. Five species occur in lakes and streams of central and eastern states. Most are valued as game fish and are caught by trolling or casting, with spoons or spinners. They are good eating, though somewhat bony.

Northern Pike can be recognized by their scaling, which covers the entirety of the cheeks but only the upper half of the gill covers. It is caught commercially, but is much more important as a game fish. Sportsmen try for it with flashy lures or live minnows.

Muskellunge is the largest pike. Though not much larger than the Northern Pike, it is considered a fiercer fighter and a better game fish. Lower cheeks and lower gill covers lack scales. Body markings show regional variations in the pattern of the dark spots or bars.

Grass Pickerel (Redfin Pickerel) is smaller and has cheeks and gill covers completely scaled. It is the commonest pickerel of small streams in the Mississippi Valley. The eastern form, Maine to Alabama, with a shorter snout, is called the Redfin Pickerel.

Chain Pickerel, often found with bass in shallow lakes and clear streams, has cheeks and gill covers completely scaled. Occurs from New England south to Florida and Texas.

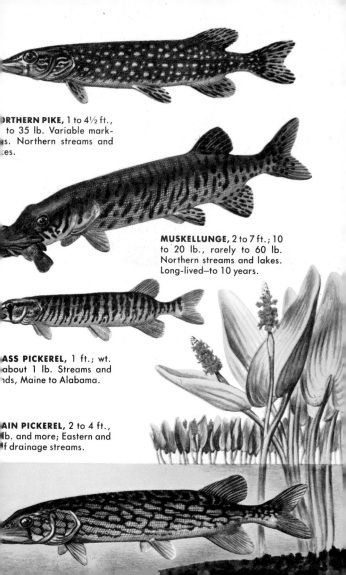

NORTHERN PIKE, 1 to 4½ ft., to 35 lb. Variable markings. Northern streams and lakes.

MUSKELLUNGE, 2 to 7 ft.; 10 to 20 lb., rarely to 60 lb. Northern streams and lakes. Long-lived—to 10 years.

GRASS PICKEREL, 1 ft.; wt. about 1 lb. Streams and ponds, Maine to Alabama.

CHAIN PICKEREL, 2 to 4 ft., 4 lb. and more; Eastern and Gulf drainage streams.

BANDED KILLIFISH, 3 to 4 in. Common in northern part of Mississippi basin.

SHEEPSHEAD MINNOW, 3 in. A heavier fish, which feeds mainly on aquatic animals.

MOSQUITOFISH, 2 in. The male *Gambusia* is much smaller than the female.

KILLIFISH and Topminnows are often called minnows, but the term is more correctly used for smaller relatives of the carp (pp. 57-59). Killifish are small (2 to 4 in.) with long, somewhat compressed bodies, small mouths, and projecting lower jaws. Tails are not forked; scales are large. These fish live in ponds, streams, ditches, and salt marshes throughout the United States, feeding on insect larvae, crustaceans, and small water plants. Some feed on wrigglers and are therefore of value in mosquito control. Mosquitofish *(Gambusia)* retain eggs in their bodies and bear their young alive. Many species breed throughout the summer.

MUMMICHOG, 5 in. Common in eastern coastal streams, marshes, and tide pools.

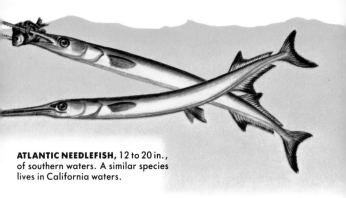

ATLANTIC NEEDLEFISH, 12 to 20 in., of southern waters. A similar species lives in California waters.

NEEDLEFISHES and HALFBEAKS are marine fishes closely related to the flyingfishes (pp. 68-69). Note the similar unbalanced tails, longer at the bottom. All species live in warmer waters. Needlefish have long bodies and very long, toothed jaws. They live at the surface and there feed on small fish. Some species grow to 5 ft., as the Houndfish of Florida waters. Halfbeaks, as their name indicates, have only the lower jaws extended. These smaller fishes rarely grow to 2 ft. long; they prefer even warmer waters than needlefishes. Other species of needlefishes and halfbeaks occur, but not too commonly, in waters off southern California.

tail of Ballyhoo

HALFBEAK, about 12 in., of south Atlantic shores. The Ballyhoo is similar but has a tail shaped more like that of the Needlefish.

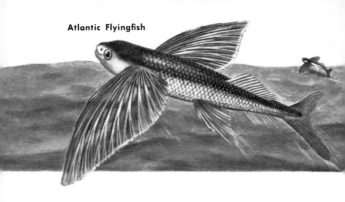

Atlantic Flyingfish

FLYINGFISHES are oceanic species often seen skittering near boats. They leave the water primarily to escape from larger fishes such as tunas and mackerels, which feed on them mainly. The Flyingfish does not actually fly. It taxis along the surface, vibrating its tail in the water; then it uses the winglike fins to glide upward, dropping down when momentum is exhausted. Often it takes to the air a second or third time without re-entering the water. Some species have the two pectoral fins enlarged; others have both pectoral and pelvic fins developed for "flight." The former are known as Two-winged, the latter as Four-winged, Flyingfishes. All species frequent warmer seas, but may appear halfway up our Atlantic and Pacific coasts. They deposit eggs, covered with long silky threads, in kelp beds, or attach them to any floating object.

The Atlantic and the Margined are two of the best-known Atlantic species. The California Flyingfish is similar to these. The Blackwing Flyingfish (reported to "fly" 500 ft. or more) is found in both the Atlantic and Pacific. Several species have barbels when immature but all lose them before maturity. Most species average 7 to 12 in. in length.

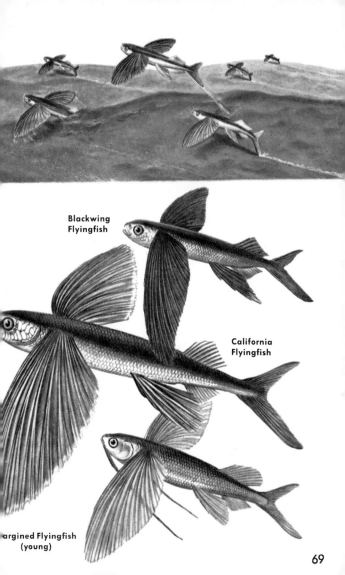

Blackwing
Flyingfish

California
Flyingfish

argined Flyingfish
(young)

69

Massachusetts' "Sacred Cod"

ATLANTIC COD stimulated the settlement of New England, fostered shipbuilding, and had other influences on early American history. In testimony of this, a large gilded pine Codfish was hung in the Massachusetts State House in 1784 and is still there.

While Cod weighing up to 200 lb. have been taken, they average 10 to 25 lb. About 83 million pounds of Cod are caught annually. Cod feed mainly on mollusks, crabs, starfish, worms, squid, and small fish. Some Cod migrate south in winter and spawn at that time; others move to deeper water. Large females produce three to five million eggs. Small Cod, prepared in strips for cooking, is called Scrod.

The Pacific Cod, caught from Oregon north, has become more important than the Atlantic Cod. In 1950, Pacific catches were too insignificant to be listed. In 1985, more than 120 million pounds of Pacific Cod were taken, compared to the 83 million for the Atlantic.

The Burbot, the only fresh-water member of the Cod family, is found in northern streams and lakes, often in deep water. A single barbel on the chin creates the mistaken idea that it is a catfish. The Burbot is a food fish, often caught in traps.

Burbot

**Atlantic Cod
red phase**

green phase

egg hatches in 10-40 days

just hatched

larva at about 2-3 weeks

**DEVELOPMENT STAGES
OF THE COD**

young—4-6 months old

71

ATLANTIC TOMCOD and POLLOCK are both in the Cod family. The Tomcod is small, rarely over 15 in. long, 1 to 1½ lb., and looks much like a young Atlantic Cod (p. 71). Note that the tip of the ventral fin is long and tapering. Living close to shore, Tomcod feed on crustaceans and small fish. They are often caught in bays and occasionally in streams. Tomcods are good eating but not important as food fish. Color is variable, usually dull green above, white or yellowish below. Pacific Tomcod are taken in small numbers north of San Francisco.

The Atlantic Pollock is a cool-water fish found on both sides of the North Atlantic. It grows to 3 ft., weighing up to 30 lb. Over 40 million pounds are caught annually, chiefly in otter trawls similar to the kind illustrated at the bottom of p. 74. The similar Walleye Pollock, found chiefly in Alaska, was of negligible importance in 1950. Since the remarkable development of the Alaskan fishery, the take of the Walleye Pollock has increased to 93 million pounds, more than doubling that of its Atlantic relative.

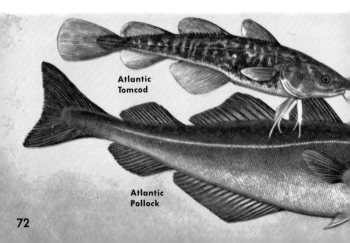

Atlantic
Tomcod

Atlantic
Pollock

HADDOCK, 30 years ago, was the top-ranking food fish. It has dropped drastically, from 100 million pounds to 26 million pounds taken annually—mostly marketed as frozen fish. Finnan haddie is a lightly smoked Haddock. On the Georges and other banks, Haddock

New England fishing banks

are more plentiful than Cod. They live in deeper water than Cod, though rarely deeper than 100 fathoms (600 ft.). Haddock are strictly bottom feeders, taking many kinds of mollusks, small crabs, worms, and other invertebrates. They are found also in colder European waters.

Haddock is distinguished from Cod by having a black lateral line, and a dark patch on each side above the pectoral fin. It is smaller than Cod but larger than Tomcod. It occasionally reaches 35 in., weighs up to 30 lb. Haddock mature when 3 to 4 years old.

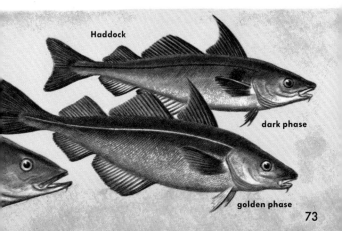

Haddock

dark phase

golden phase

Silver Hake

LINGS and HAKES are Cod-like fishes, of considerable importance in commercial fisheries. The Silver Hake, also known as Whiting, lacks the chin barbels of the true hakes or lings. It also has larger scales. This slender fish is a swift, strong swimmer which preys on shrimp and smaller fish. It is found at all depths down to about 300 fathoms but prefers somewhat warmer water than the Cod. With the advent of quick-freezing it has become an important food fish. The Silver Hake spawns in summer; the transparent eggs hatch in about 2 days. Adults mature in 3 years and rarely grow more than 2 ft. long, weighing 5 lb. (average 1 to 2 lb.). Large runs occur in spring and fall. A close relative is common in the deeper waters of the Gulf of Mexico.

The lings include several very similar species. All are more slender than Cod and have two dorsal fins, one short

otter trawl for hake

White Hake

and the other long. The tail is weak and rounded. All are bottom fish, feeding on crustaceans and small fish, but not on mollusks. They are night feeders and may be caught by line, though most of the commercial catch is made with otter trawls.

White Hake or Mud Hake, the largest species, gets to be 4 ft. long; weight to 40 lb.; average about 8 lb. Its large mouth extends back beyond the eyes.

The Squirrel or Red Hake (or Ling) is smaller than the others, averaging 1 to 3 lb., but is otherwise very similar to the White Hake. Its mouth, slightly smaller, extends only as far back as the pupil of the eye.

White Hake   Red Hake

Southern Hake, or Florida Ling, is still smaller—usually less than 1 ft. long. It lives at medium depths but comes inshore during cold weather.

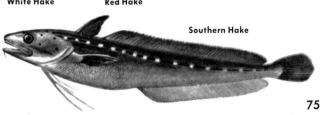

Southern Hake

HOGCHOKER or Broad Sole is one of a group of smaller flatfishes (p. 78) which include the European species that provides filet of sole. In the United States we get filet of sole from flounders.

Soles prefer warm, shallow water with a sandy or muddy bottom. Several Atlantic and one Pacific species occur.

FLATFISH

FLATFISHES form a unique and widespread group that includes about 130 American species, common in both Atlantic and Pacific. Some are valuable food fish; some are prized by sportsmen; all have developed a most unusual body form adapted to life on the bottom. As shown below, the transparent larvae soon change in form, and the eyes migrate to one side of the head (either left or right, depending on the species). The bottom side of the flatfish is white or pale; the top side varies in color, and all species can adjust their color and pattern to the bottom on which they live. All have a single long dorsal and anal fin, without spines.

There are two groups of flatfishes. The Soles have small eyes, placed close together, and a small twisted mouth with few or no teeth. They are generally smaller fish. The Flounders are a much larger group and include the Flounders, Flukes, Halibuts, Turbots, and Dabs. Detailed identification may be difficult; it depends on number of rays in fins, number of gill rakers, and other characteristics not easily observed.

egg larva—
newly hatched

SMOOTH FLOUNDER (right), a northern fish, prefers muddy bottoms in cold, shallow water. It breeds in winter. It is unusual in that the female has smoother scales and shorter pectoral fins than the male. Note the straight lateral line and the smooth area between the eyes.

SOUTHERN FLOUNDER is an important food and game fish. Large numbers are caught by trawls. Anglers get them near shore during summer. In winter, the fish seek deeper water to spawn. The Summer Flounder, which is found from Maine to South Carolina, is similar in appearance and habits.

AMERICAN PLAICE, or Sand Dab (left), is common at 20 to 100 fathoms on muddy or sandy bottoms. Up to 6 million lb. are taken annually. Length to 30 in. (average, 18 in.), weight, to 14 lb. (average, 7 lb.). Feeds on sea urchins, sand dollars, and other bottom-dwellers.

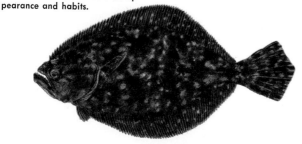

swims upright—eye on each side

swims on one side—eyes on the other

STARRY FLOUNDER is a common and abundant Pacific flatfish found from mid-California north to Alaska and west to Asia. One of the most attractive flounders, it is as good eating as its drabber relatives. Feeds mainly on worms and crustaceans; weight up to 15 or 20 lb.

CALIFORNIA HALIBUT may grow 3 ft. long and up to 60 lb., though the average size is much smaller. Note the small eyes, separated by a large flat area. The lateral line swings into a high arch near the pectoral fins. Found all year, but mainly in spring, from San Francisco south.

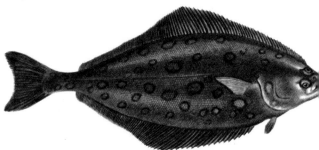

ATLANTIC HALIBUT, large, large-mouthed flatfish marked by a concave tail, are northern fish but avoid very cold water. They feed mainly on other fish. Halibut may run from 400 to 600 lb. and to over 8 ft. More usual are those of 20 to 100 lb. which are caught offshore at 100 to 400 fathoms. Pacific Halibut are very similar.

STICKLEBACKS are a family of small fishes, distributed widely around the world in northern waters. Some are fresh-water, some marine, and some are at home in either element. Sticklebacks range from 1½ to 4 in. long. They feed on fish eggs, larvae and small crustaceans. In spring and summer, when they spawn, the male is brightly colored and very jealous. Fights between males are common. Each male builds a round nest of water plants held together by mucus threads. In it, several females in succession may deposit their eggs. These are guarded by the male, who also protects the young after they hatch—in about 10 days.

The Brook Stickleback is a fresh-water species found in northern lakes and streams. It is identified by 5 or 6 spines in front of the dorsal fin. The Ninespine Stickleback, of both fresh and brackish water, is similar, but with more spines on the back. The Threespine Stickleback, of similar habitat, is also found in Europe. The male builds a nest using a sticky skin secretion and bits of vegetation.

Brook Stickleback

male

Threespine Stickleback

female in nest

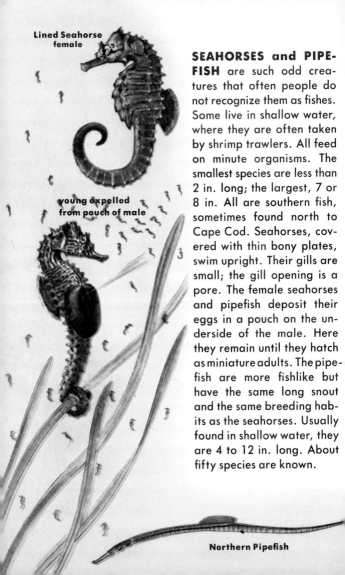

Lined Seahorse female

young expelled from pouch of male

SEAHORSES and PIPE-FISH are such odd creatures that often people do not recognize them as fishes. Some live in shallow water, where they are often taken by shrimp trawlers. All feed on minute organisms. The smallest species are less than 2 in. long; the largest, 7 or 8 in. All are southern fish, sometimes found north to Cape Cod. Seahorses, covered with thin bony plates, swim upright. Their gills are small; the gill opening is a pore. The female seahorses and pipefish deposit their eggs in a pouch on the underside of the male. Here they remain until they hatch as miniature adults. The pipefish are more fishlike but have the same long snout and the same breeding habits as the seahorses. Usually found in shallow water, they are 4 to 12 in. long. About fifty species are known.

Northern Pipefish

Striped Mullet

MULLETS and SILVERSIDES introduce the spiny-rayed fishes, which include most species through p. 131 and a few others. The mullets are blunt-nosed, warm-water fishes of both Atlantic and Pacific. They are common in shallow water, where small schools may leap in unison when frightened. Mullets feed on aquatic plants and mud but they sometimes bite on doughballs. A good food fish, they are often netted and smoked. Of several species, the Striped Mullet is most common; it grows to 2 ft.

Silversides are shore fish, but much smaller in size. Like Mullets they have two dorsal fins, but also a silvery stripe on the side. The Inland Silverside (a close relative of the Pacific Whitebait) is found from New England south. It rarely grows over 3 in. long. The Brook Silverside is a similar, fresh-water species.

Inland Silverside

Brook Silverside

CALIFORNIA GRUNION is a larger and better known relative of the silverside. This fine Pacific fish, known from Monterey south, comes to the beach during the highest tides to spawn and lay its eggs in the sand. Such times are the occasions for all-night Grunion parties. As the fish are cast ashore by the waves, they are grabbed bare-handed for cooking on the beach or later at home. These slender, silvery Grunions, mistakenly called Smelts, are 5 to 8 in. long. Some are caught commercially in round-haul nets.

Topsmelt and Jacksmelt are actually silversides, not Smelts. They are caught along the California coast and are close relatives of the Grunion. Jacksmelts are taken by anglers and also form a major part of the California "smelt" fisheries; length, 10 to 22 in.

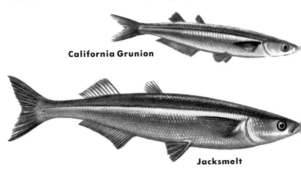

California Grunion

Jacksmelt

Pacific Barracuda

Great Barracuda

BARRACUDAS are the large, slender "tigers" of tropical seas, widely known because they are both ferocious and excellent food and game fishes. Barracudas strike at anything bright or moving. They may occur in shallow water; and the largest, the Great Barracuda, is often accused of being dangerous to swimmers. Some evidence of this danger has recently been confirmed, but the fact remains that barracudas are much less dangerous than sharks. The Great Barracuda grows to 10 ft. long, though any over 5 ft. are rare. The Pacific Barracuda is usually not over 4 ft. long and weighs 10 to 12 lb. The Northern Barracuda and other smaller species are not dangerous.

Barracuda feed on smaller fish. They are caught by trolling or with live bait, and are also netted in commercial fishing. They spawn in summer but may spawn twice a year.

83

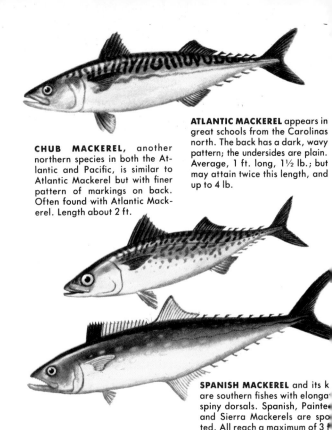

CHUB MACKEREL, another northern species in both the Atlantic and Pacific, is similar to Atlantic Mackerel but with finer pattern of markings on back. Often found with Atlantic Mackerel. Length about 2 ft.

ATLANTIC MACKEREL appears in great schools from the Carolinas north. The back has a dark, wavy pattern; the undersides are plain. Average, 1 ft. long, 1½ lb.; but may attain twice this length, and up to 4 lb.

SPANISH MACKEREL and its k are southern fishes with elonga spiny dorsals. Spanish, Painte and Sierra Mackerels are spo ted. All reach a maximum of 3 and 10 or 15 lb.

MACKEREL and their kin are easily recognized by their deeply forked tails, which narrow greatly as they join the body. Both dorsal and anal fins have small finlets behind them; and finally, the mackerels all have a sleek, streamlined form with smooth, almost scaleless skins. Their

KING MACKEREL or Cero is the only member of the Spanish Mackerel genus that lacks spots. Like other mackerels, it feeds on small fish and squid. It is found north to the Carolinas. It can weigh up to 60 lb.

WAHOO is a more solitary mackerel of the Gulf Stream and warm-water reefs. Note long dorsal fin and wavy bands, extending well past the lateral line. Averages 15 to 20 lb.—sometimes much larger.

iridescence makes them more attractive than many other species. These swift fishes usually travel in schools, which migrate widely. They live along shore and far at sea. In this group are the world's best game fishes and fishes of high commercial value.

TUNA, ALBACORE, and BONITO are large members of the mackerel family. A few are no larger than the mackerels on the preceding pages, but the giant tunas are the largest of the bony fishes. These larger mackerels also swim in schools. They migrate in irregular paths and

LITTLE TUNNY or False Albacore is a fish of open waters frequently caught and called "bonito" by sportsmen. Found north to Cape Cod in summer. 2 to 3 ft., 10 lb. Feeds on flyingfishes.

SKIPJACK TUNA or Oceanic Bonito prefers warmer waters on Atlantic and Pacific coasts. Note stripes on underside and that the lateral lines curve down sharply; 2 ft. long; 20 lb.; few larger.

ALBACORE live all along the coast, but are more abundant in the south. This is the "whitemeat tuna" important in commercial fishing. Atlantic and Pacific species are identical.

ATLANTIC BONITO is not so important in commercial fisheries. A good sport fish, more abundant in summer. A very similar and slightly larger Pacific species grows to 40 in. and 25 lb.

schedules. All feed on such pelagic fish as mackerels, herring, and sardines, and also squid. All are valuable food fishes, and tuna are famous game. These fish and their kin range the tropical and temperate seas. California tuna boats fish as far south as Peru.

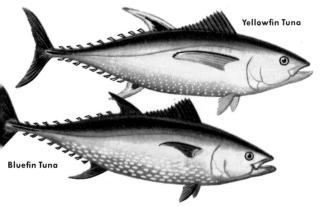

Yellowfin Tuna

Bluefin Tuna

BLUEFIN TUNA are represented by two very similar species, one on the Atlantic and one on the Pacific. The Atlantic species is larger: 200- to 500-lb. fishes are commonly caught. The record is about 1,496 lb. Tuna come toward shore and move north in summer, following a more plentiful food supply.

YELLOWFIN TUNA and the Skipjack are the principal species caught at sea by the California tuna fleet. Large numbers of Yellowfin have recently been found in the Gulf of Mexico. More southerly in its range than the Bluefin, this tuna is also smaller— up to 500 lb., usually 125 lb. or less. An excellent game fish.

MARLINS rank highest on the sportsman's list. All are open-sea fishes which feed on other fish. Of three species living in North American waters, the Blue Marlin is best known. This, the largest marlin (up to about 1,000 lb.), is found in the Gulf Stream as far north as Long Island. Its upper jaw is extended into a long pike, used in clubbing small fish as it feeds. The ventral fins are reduced to a pair of long filaments. The Striped Marlin of the Pacific barely enters California waters from the south and is caught near the Santa Barbara Islands. It is smaller than the Blue Marlin—up to 300 or 400 lb. Its back is marked by about a dozen gray stripes. The White Marlin is paler in color and much smaller—rarely weighing more than 100 lb. It lives in our Atlantic waters, moving northward as spring advances.

Blue Marlin

Striped Marlin

White Marlin

Sailfish

SAILFISH are found as far north as Cape Cod on the Atlantic and as far north as Monterey on the Pacific. The two subspecies, one in the Atlantic and one in the Pacific, are almost identical, except that the Pacific subspecies may average up to 100 lb. and the Atlantic Sailfish comes nearer 60 lb. Both have a high, wide dorsal fin, which gives the fish its name; also small scales embedded in the skin, as in marlins. Sailfish lack finlets. They often appear in schools chasing Mackerel, Menhaden, and smaller fishes. Sailfish have oily flesh and are not a favorite food, but they are prized as game. They are usually caught by trolling in deep water. When hooked, a sailfish will leap, twist, and "tail-walk" on the water in an effort to shake loose. Sportsmen often release the fish they have landed.

SWORDFISH, bearing a long, sharp, broad "sword," are quite distinct from the marlins and sailfish with their round pointed beaks. Swordfish are found in warmer waters of the Pacific and Atlantic; they move as far north as Nova Scotia by the end of the summer. Often bask at the surface and are not easily disturbed. Swordfish grow up to 15 ft. long and weigh up to 1,000 lb., but fish even half that size are considered large. An excellent food fish and prized game fish, taken with line or by harpoon. Swordfish prefer deeper, offshore waters of the Gulf Stream. Feed on small fish.

Marlin bill

Swordfish sword

INSHORE LIZARDFISH represents a southern family. Lives on sandy bottoms; feeds on smaller fish. Length to 1 ft.

DOLPHIN or Dorado should not be confused with the mammal of the same name (p. 152). These fish are unusual in several ways: their odd, blunt heads and tapering bodies with a long dorsal fin; their magnificent color, which varies from fish to fish and which changes in waves on the living Dolphin; and their unusual speed. Dolphins are one of the fastest fishes. They live at the surface, chasing and feeding on flyingfishes and other small kinds. Mainly a southern fish, the Dolphin has been found north to New England in summer. It is occasionally reported along the Pacific also. Maximum size is up to 6 ft. long, weight 60 lb.; usually it is much smaller. Dolphins frequently leap from the water when hunting smaller fish or when they are chased by something larger. The high forehead is characteristic of the male.

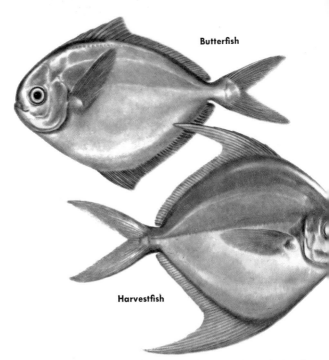

Butterfish

Harvestfish

BUTTERFISH are small (6 to 9 in. long, weight ½ lb., occasionally larger) food fish widely distributed in open waters of the Atlantic. They live in schools on sandy bottoms close to shore. Butterfish spawn in summer, disappearing from northern waters in the winter. Nets yield about 7 million pounds annually. Butterfish and Harvestfish represent the harvestfish family in the Atlantic.

HARVESTFISH live more to the south than Butterfish and are not as important as food fish. Their size is similar. Note the differences in the fins. The California Pompano (not a true pompano) is a common Pacific harvestfish.

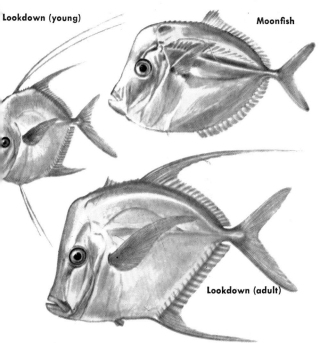

Lookdown (young)

Moonfish

Lookdown (adult)

MOONFISH and LOOKDOWN belong to the family of jacks (pp. 94-95), mackerel-like fishes of warmer waters. These two species are more flattened than other jacks. The Moonfish is the more common of the two and is netted in the south as a food fish. Both fishes average about 9 in. long and weigh about half a pound, though they may get larger. The Lookdown is similar to the Moonfish but has elongated dorsal and anal fins and an even blunter head. The young have long filaments on dorsal and ventral fins. Lookdowns are caught locally in channels and near ledges. They put up a good fight and are fine eating.

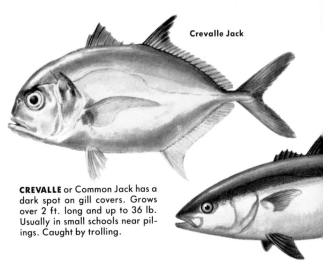

Crevalle Jack

CREVALLE or Common Jack has a dark spot on gill covers. Grows over 2 ft. long and up to 36 lb. Usually in small schools near pilings. Caught by trolling.

JACKS and POMPANO represent a large and important family of open-sea fishes. Note the deeply forked tails on thin stalks, often strengthened by heavy keels, with knife-sharp ridges. Jacks and their kin prefer warm waters, though in summer some may be found all along the Atlantic Coast. A few species occur on our Pacific Coast. Many jacks are excellent food and game fish. "Pompano en papillote" (cooked in paper) is a famous delicacy.

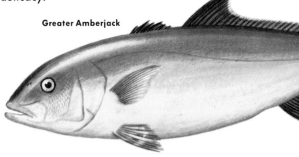

Greater Amberjack

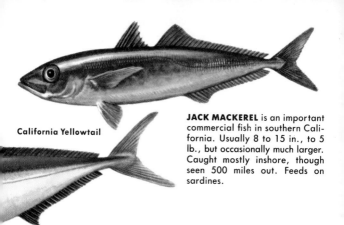

California Yellowtail

JACK MACKEREL is an important commercial fish in southern California. Usually 8 to 15 in., to 5 lb., but occasionally much larger. Caught mostly inshore, though seen 500 miles out. Feeds on sardines.

CALIFORNIA YELLOWTAIL (above) is streamlined like the mackerels. Schools are found on our southern Pacific coast. A popular game fish. Weight to 40 lb.

FLORIDA POMPANO (below, left) is a prized food and game fish, most common south of the Carolinas in inlets and near shore. It is also caught at buoys or at offshore oil rigs. Weight about 2 lb.

Florida
Pompano

Permit

GREATER AMBERJACK (left) is larger than the Common Jack—averaging 12 lb., occasionally reaching 100. Common off Florida; rarer farther north. Feeds, like other jacks, on smaller fishes.

PERMIT resembles the pompano and is sometimes called Round Pompano. Length about 1 ft.; weight about 2 lb. Found in inlets of most southern waters with pompanos.

PILOTFISH is a slender jack, rarely growing over 2 ft. long. It is widespread in warmer waters and is occasionally found north to Cape Cod. Pilotfish prefer deeper water, often following ships or large sharks and feeding on scraps these bigger fish leave behind. They do not lead sharks to food, as some stories have it.

Pilotfish

BLUEFISH (below) is in a family by itself. It resembles pompano in some aspects, though it may be more closely related to the sea basses. Bluefish are excellent food and game fish, found in both deep and shallow water and caught by trolling, nets, or seines. Length to about 30 in., weight 10 to 12 lb.; rarely larger.

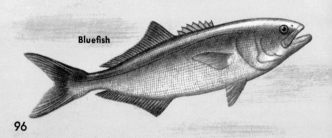

Bluefish

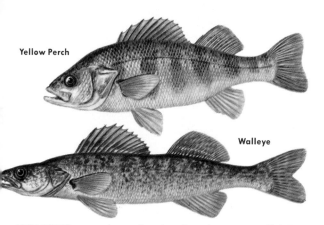

Yellow Perch

Walleye

PERCHES are a large family of medium to small fishes also found in Europe. The Yellow Perch (to 12 in. and 1 lb.) is best known. It is abundant in lakes and large streams, feeding on insects, crayfish, and small fish. Perch spawn in spring; lower fins then reddish. Walleye is a larger, darker perch (up to 10 lb.), fished commercially, and a popular game fish, though becoming less common. Eastern Sauger, similar to Walleye but slenderer and smaller (12 to 14 in.), often occurs with it.

RAINBOW DARTER (2 to 3 in.). Males attractive with red on fins. Prefer larger creeks with gravel bottoms.

JOHNNY DARTER (2 to 3 in. long) belongs to a large group of small perchlike fishes of brooks and lakes.

Rainbow Darter

Johnny Darter

SACRAMENTO PERCH—only native Western sunfish. Color variable. 1 ft.

BASSES, often called the finest of fresh-water game fish, are of the sunfish family, which includes 30-odd species in warmer lakes and ponds. All members of the family have a single dorsal fin, the spiny and soft dorsals being continuous. All build nests in which the male guards eggs and fry. Sunfishes are widely distributed and some have been transplanted outside of their native eastern waters.

Largemouth Bass, when young, has on the sides a dark stripe, which disappears as the fish matures. The mouth is large and extends back beyond the eye. Foods are mainly crayfish and small fish. Largemouth and Smallmouth Bass are top game fish. Both have been introduced west of the Rockies. To 8 lb.; larger in south.

Smallmouth Bass differs from the Largemouth in having faint vertical bars on the sides, and a mouth that extends to, but not beyond, the pupil of the eye. Maximum weight about 6 lb. The Smallmouth prefers deeper and cooler water than the Largemouth. It does not range as far south and is absent from Gulf Coast streams.

Spotted Bass is intermediate between the Largemouth and the Smallmouth in mouth size, body size, and fin shape. It has a lateral stripe and many small dark spots over the sides. Fingerlings are easily distinguished by their bright orange tail.

Largemouth Bass

Smallmouth Bass

Spotted Bass

SUNFISHES or Bream are small members of the sunfish family (see p. 98). These favorites in lakes, streams, and ponds include over a dozen species, all easy to catch.

Bluegill, one of the largest sunfishes, sometimes weighs over 1 lb. — averages ¼ lb. Color variable, usually with faint bars, and dark lobes extending back from the gill covers. Found in central states and as far west as Colorado. Introduced in Pacific coast states, they thrive in farm ponds and lakes.

Longear Sunfish is so named because of the long flaps or lobes that are extensions of its gill covers. This sunfish rarely gets over 8 in. long— usually not over 6. The brilliantly colored Longear shows bright orange and blue in irregular patterns. One of the two commonest sunfishes (Green Sunfish is the other) of small creeks in the Mississippi Valley.

Bluegill

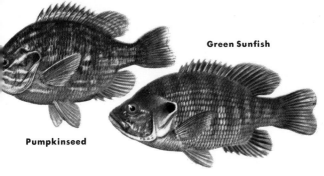

Green Sunfish

Pumpkinseed

Pumpkinseed, or Common Sunfish, has a less regular color pattern than the Bluegill but usually has strong orange and blue stripes on the cheeks, and a tell-tale red spot marks the back of the gill covers. Rarely over 8 in. long; weight to 1 lb. Often found in schools on weedy margins of ponds and lakes, feeding on insects and small crustaceans.

Green Sunfish, one of the smaller sunfishes, rarely gets over 6 in. long. Probably the most common sunfish, it is similar to the Pumpkinseed but lacks the red spot on the gill covers. There are black spots at the base of the soft dorsal and anal fins. Found throughout the central states and as far west as Colorado, it has been introduced along the Pacific.

Longear Sunfish

Redear Sunfish

Redear Sunfish or Shellcracker (above) is common in the Mississippi basin from Illinois south, and most abundant in the south; sometimes in brackish water. It grows a bit larger than other species (up to 10 in.) and has been transplanted outside its range. Note the red tip on the lobe of the gill covers; this gives the fish one of its common names.

Warmouth ranges through the Mississippi basin to the Gulf in lakes, ponds, and large streams. It feeds on insects and small fish and, like other sunfishes, takes the hook readily. Grows 8 to 10 in. long and usually not over 1 lb. It is a nest builder. Warmouth has a large mouth like that of the Rock Bass, but it has only three anal spines and more conspicuous lines back of the eye.

Rock Bass is difficult to picture, since it changes color rapidly to blend with its surroundings. It, too, occurs in the Mississippi basin, but is more common in the cooler clear waters of the north. It spawns in late spring on gravel bottoms and under weedy banks. A good game fish, 8 to 10 in. long; often weighs over 1 lb.

Spotted Sunfish (Spotted Bream or Stumpknocker), common in southern ponds, streams, and brackish water, is a smaller sunfish, marked by small dark specks. During the breeding season, mature fish develop a brick red color. Length, 6 to 8 in.; weight usually 8 to 18 oz.

Spotted Sunfish

Warmouth

Rock Bass

CRAPPIES are the largest of the sunfishes. Two species, the Black Crappie and the White Crappie, inhabit about the same range in the Mississippi valley and Great Lakes region. They have been widely transplanted elsewhere. There are slight differences in color pattern and in the dorsal spines, and the shorter snout of the Black Crappie is turned up. Both species spawn in spring when one or two years old. They feed on small water animals, insects, crustaceans, and to some extent on small fish. Crappies are easily caught through winter ice or in the spring, and make an excellent pan fish. They often grow to 12 in. long and weigh over 2 lb.

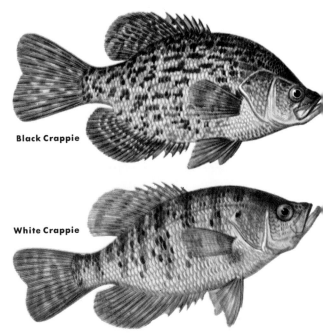

Black Crappie

White Crappie

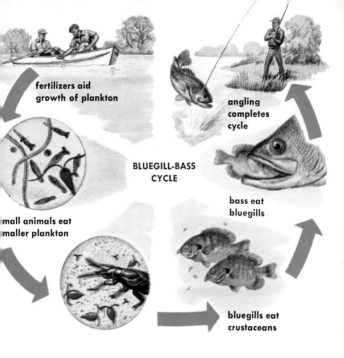

fertilizers aid
growth of plankton

angling
completes
cycle

**BLUEGILL-BASS
CYCLE**

bass eat
bluegills

mall animals eat
maller plankton

bluegills eat
crustaceans

FISH CULTIVATION in farm ponds is increasing. Over a million such ponds exist; some produce as much as 200 lb. of fish per acre. Where soil fertility and therefore the pond fertility are very low, commercial fertilizers are used to aid the growth of plankton (microscopic plant and animal life). This serves as food for crustaceans and small fishes, which are eaten by larger fishes. Too-high fertility may cause excessive and obnoxious plant growth. In the popular Bluegill-Bass combination, the problem has been to avoid excess production of bluegills, by intensive angling and netting. Detailed instructions are available from federal and most state conservation agencies.

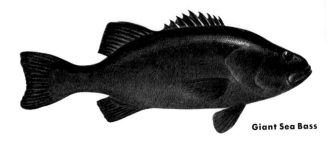

Giant Sea Bass

TEMPERATE BASSES include the White Perch which, until 1970, was placed in the same family as the sea basses (p. 108). Now the White Perch, White Bass, Yellow Bass, and Striped Bass have been found to be different enough from the sea basses to move them to the newly created family of temperate basses. Also included in this family is the Giant Sea Bass, or Pacific Jewfish, a dark, heavily built bottom fish that may weigh up to 600 lb. and attain 7 ft. or more in length. This popular game fish, found from central California south, also has some commercial importance as a food fish.

WHITE BASS, a fresh-water fish, belongs to the family of temperate basses. It lives in the larger rivers and lakes of the Mississippi Valley and in the Great Lakes. Note the silvery, striped body and divided dorsal fin. A good game fish. Length: to 18 in.

STRIPED BASS (illustrated on p. 8) is the best-known temperate bass, found from Florida to Canada but best known from New Jersey to Cape Cod. It has been successfully transplanted to the Pacific coast. The Striped Bass is

Surf fishing for Striped Bass

a superb food and game fish, growing up to 125 lb., though half that weight is more typical. In May it moves into bays or up streams to spawn. Food: fish, crabs, shrimp, and other invertebrates. White Perch is another fine temperate bass of both brackish and fresh water on the Atlantic coast.

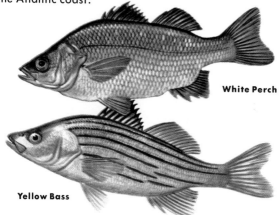

White Perch

Yellow Bass

YELLOW BASS is related and quite similar to White Bass. It rarely grows over 15 in. long. Some of the stripes on its sides are interrupted. A good game and food fish, it is found in north-central lakes and rivers, and sometimes in brackish bays.

SEA BASSES are a large and diverse family of perchlike fishes. Most species have three heavy spines before the anal fin, and one or two spines on the edge of the gill covers.

Black Sea Bass is most common from Florida to Cape Cod. This bottom fish is often found near rocks, both inshore and off, feeding on crabs, shrimp, and small fishes. Sides mottled, with narrow horizontal stripes. A superior game fish. Weight to 6 lb.; length to 18 in.

Black Sea Bass

Kelp Bass

Kelp Bass is a much smaller fish; it rarely gets to be over 2 ft. long. It is common in kelp beds, where it is frequently taken by anglers using live bait. One of the leading California sport fishes and of some commercial importance, it is caught more often in summer. It is rare north of Monterey.

JEWFISHES AND GROUPERS are large sea basses, found in southern waters of the Atlantic and the Gulf, usually on rocky bottoms and around reefs. The Warsaw Grouper, or Black Jewfish, does not occur north of the Carolinas. It reaches a length of 6 ft. and a weight of at least 500 lb. Oddly, small fish are rarer than those of the larger size. Jewfish are taken by hook and line commercially as well as for sport. The Jewfish is not found north of Florida. It, too, is a fish of rocks and reefs, though it also lives around pilings. This jewfish grows larger than the Warsaw, reaching over 600 lb. (record 693 lb., length 8 ft.). It is a sluggish fish and hence is easy prey to spear fishermen, who take them frequently. As a food fish it once had little value, but now it is becoming increasingly popular and more widely used.

Warsaw Grouper

Jewfish

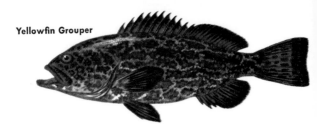

Yellowfin Grouper

YELLOWFIN GROUPER is a West Indies fish that is also found in the Florida Keys. It prefers reefs and offshore banks, where it feeds on crabs and small fishes. This handsome fish has two color phases and changes color rapidly. Grows to 18 in.; averages 3 lb.

Red Grouper

RED GROUPER ranges as far north as the Carolinas. Along with the Black Grouper it forms the bulk of the commercial grouper catch. Food similar to that of other groupers. This common species grows to 50 lb.

BLACK GROUPER, a West Indies species, is also common on the northern Gulf Coast. It is abundant in Florida Keys; occasionally ranges to Massachusetts. Grows 3 ft. long, up to 50 lb.

Black Grouper

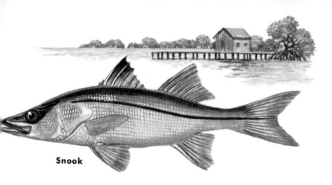

Snook

SNOOKS are widely distributed in tropical seas. One species is common off Florida and along the Texas coast. Pacific species do not quite touch U.S. waters. Snooks are found close to shore, in bays and inlets, often going upstream into fresh water. They are fine game fish and are excellent eating also. Snooks are related to the sea basses (pp. 108-110) but have longer, thinner bodies, a straight lower profile, and a projecting lower jaw. Average weight about 4 lb., occasionally up to 50; length up to 4 ft.

Tripletail

TRIPLETAIL gets its name from the prominent dorsal and anal fins, which make the fish look as if it had three tails. Common in Atlantic north to Cape Cod; more common in the south. Feeds on smaller fishes. Length about 20 in.; average weight over 10 lb.

SNAPPERS are another group of tropical fishes which find their way along the Gulf and Atlantic coasts, sometimes as far north as Cape Cod. Snappers usually aggregate on offshore "lumps," though some species of less commercial importance are found near shore. They feed on crabs, shrimp, and small fish.

Schoolmaster, of Florida waters, is found around wharves and along the reefs. Grows about 18 in. long; weight 2 to 3 lb., occasionally up to 8. A common species, marked by light bars and yellow fins.

Gray Snapper, also called Mangrove Snapper, is often found around mangroves in the Florida Keys. Reputed to be one of the best-tasting snappers, it feeds largely on crabs. Occasionally found as far north as New Jersey. Average length is about 18 in.; average weight about 2-3 lb., but specimens of 15 to 18 lb. have been caught.

Red Snapper is a famous food fish found mainly in the Gulf of Mexico, but also along the Atlantic Coast as far north as Long Island. It is usually caught with hand lines. Pensacola and Caribbean Red Snapper have recently been shown to be the same species. Length, to 3 ft.

Schoolmaster

Red Snapper

Gray Snapper

Yellowtail Snapper is a small snapper with a big reputation as a tasty fish. It is rarely found north of Florida, where it lives along reefs and in inlets. Identified by a deeply forked tail, yellow fins, and a yellow stripe along the sides to the tail. Length to 2 ft.; average length under 1 ft.

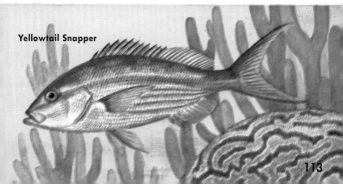

Yellowtail Snapper

PORKFISH A small, brightly colored grunt of Florida waters; 1 to 2 lb.

GRUNTS are closely related to snappers but have fewer teeth and brightly colored mouths. Most are small, all are tropical. Common in the Atlantic. The California Sargo is a common grunt of Pacific waters.

White Grunt, common from the West Indies to the Carolinas and a favorite food fish, has four rows of enlarged scales above lateral line. Average length, 1 ft.; average weight, 1 lb.—rarely up to 18 in. long and 4 lb. Found on shallow, sandy bottoms.

Bluestriped Grunt is marked as its name indicates with narrow, horizontal blue stripes. Fins are yellowish, inside of mouth red. Lacks the large scales of the White Grunt. This handsome, tasty grunt grows to about 18 in. and up to 4 lb. Common in the Florida Keys. Easily caught.

Tomtate is a small grunt, not more than 8 or 10 in. long. It has the same range as the White Grunt. Usually found in shallow water, around rocks and docks, feeding on whatever animal life it encounters.

Pigfish occasionally finds its way to Long Island Sound and westward in the Gulf to Texas. Most common in south U.S. Atlantic coastal waters, where it is an important food fish. Habits similar to Tomtate's. Note diagonal stripes on back. To about 14 in. and 3 lb.

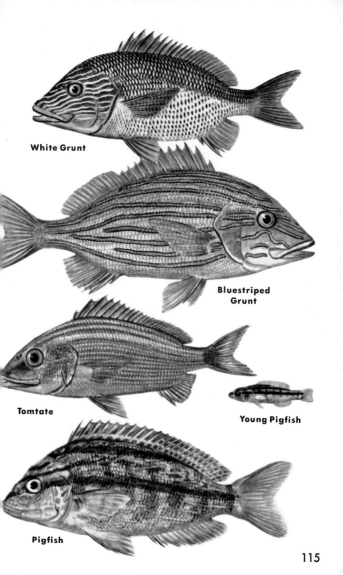

White Grunt

Bluestriped Grunt

Tomtate

Young Pigfish

Pigfish

115

Scup

PORGIES are small-mouthed fishes with strong jaw teeth, adapted to feeding on shellfish and crustaceans. Scup or Porgy (from the Carolinas to Cape Cod, on sandy bottoms) is a sport and food fish. Length, about 16 in.; weight, 1 to 2 lb. The northern and southern forms are the same species. Sheepshead Porgy, common and large, affords sport to spear fishermen. Found south of Chesapeake Bay and into the Gulf. Not related to California Sheepshead (p. 130). Of other southern species, the Jolt-head is largest (up to 10 lb.) and best known; so called because it jolts and pushes shellfish off pilings when feeding.

SHEEPSHEAD PORGY, a bottom feeder; up to 20 to 30 lb. Dark bands most conspicuous in young.

Jolthead Porgy

Pinfish

PINFISH is a porgy; also called Pinfish Bream, or Sailor's Choice. (The last name is applied to two grunts also.) Found from Cape Cod south and common along the Gulf in bays, inlets, and around piers. Grows 6 to 10 in. long, less than 1 lb. A fine-flavored fish.

OPALEYE, also called Green Perch or Catalina Perch, is the only common member of a Pacific family and a favorite sport fish for surf casters. Maximum size about 20 in. long and 6 lb. The young have whitish blotches on each side of the back. Opaleye is found from Monterey Bay south to lower California.

Opaleye

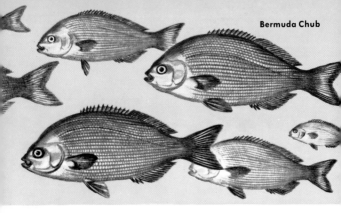

Bermuda Chub

CHUBS are small-mouthed fishes somewhat like porgies. They are known to follow ships at sea, probably as scavengers. The Bermuda Chub, common off Florida, is found north to Cape Cod. It weighs 3 to 4 lb., occasionally much more; has distinct light dots on dark background. Large schools are found around old wrecks and along reefs, feeding on animal and vegetable matter.

MOJARRAS are small tropical fish, rarely over a foot long. They extend their jaws into a long tube (as shown below) as they feed on whatever plant or animal material is available. There are many American species, all silvery. They are among the commonest Atlantic shore fishes and are also found on the Pacific Coast. More abundant in warmer waters, mojarras are seldom over 6 in. long.

Silver Jenny

mouth
projected

Weakfish

Spotted Seatrout

WEAKFISH and SEATROUTS are best known of the croakers, a family of temperate- and warm-water fishes that frequent shallows. Also called Squeteagues, Weakfish are important food and game fish along the Atlantic coast. Their weak mouths tear when hooked. Large schools move north in late spring, feeding on small fishes and invertebrates. Length, 3 ft.; weight, 12 lb. The Spotted Seatrout or "speckle trout" is similar but has dark spots on fins and body, and a more southerly range. Length, 2 ft.; weight, 8 lb.

WHITE SEABASS, a Pacific croaker, relative of the Weakfish, lives as far north as Puget Sound. Found inshore, often in kelp beds, feeding on small fish and crustaceans. Weight to 60 lb. An important commercial fish.

White Seabass

ATLANTIC CROAKER is the common species of the croaker family. It feeds on mollusks, crustaceans, and small fishes in bays and shallow water, where it usually lives in eel grass or in oyster beds. Has small chin barbels. Occasionally caught up to Cape Cod, but more common to the south. Averages 1 lb., sometimes reaches 4 or 5 lb. Spawns offshore in late summer.

SPOTFIN CROAKER is marked by large dark spots at the base of the pectoral fins. It is often caught by Pacific Coast surf-fishers, also from docks and boats near shore. More common south of Monterey. Length, to 2 ft.; weight, to 6 lbs.

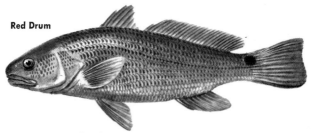

Red Drum

DRUMS are the largest and noisiest of the croakers, which make loud noises by vibrating muscles that cause their air bladders to vibrate. The Black Drum grows to over 4 ft. and weighs up to 150 lb., but averaging less than ten. Like the Sheepshead Porgy (p. 116) it feeds on mollusks. Though large and good to eat, this drum is not considered much of a game fish. The Red Drum, or Channel Bass, is an excellent sportsman's fish. Found from New York south, it feeds on small fish, shrimp, and crabs. Note its color. There may be more than one black spot at the base of the tail. This fish travels in schools and weighs 5 to 15 lb.—occasionally 50 lb. or more.

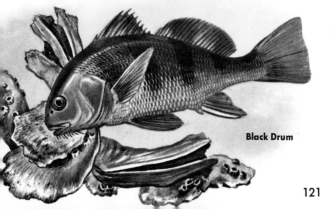

Black Drum

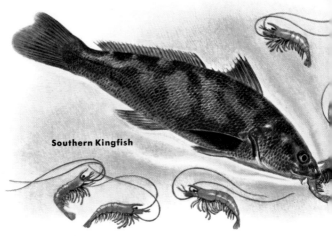

Southern Kingfish

KINGFISHES, highly prized for their food qualities, are a group of croakers found in both Atlantic and Pacific. All are somewhat similar and have a chin barbel. The Northern Kingfish, also known as Whiting, is common as far south as Maryland, where it gradually becomes rarer as the Southern Kingfish becomes commoner. Both species are bottom feeders found on sandy bottoms in fairly shallow water. The Gulf Kingfish is confined to sandy beaches from Chesapeake Bay to Texas. The Corbina, which is the Pacific counterpart of the Gulf Kingfish, is often taken by surf-casting. Kingfishes weigh 3 lb., grow to 2 ft.

California Corbina

TILEFISH are unusual fish with a most unusual history. Studies show that they thrive only at depths of 50 to 100 fathoms, and there only when the water temperature is close to 50 degrees. In this narrow range the tilefish is a bottom feeder, growing to over 3 ft. long and a weight of over 35 lb., though averaging much less. Note the fleshy flap at the top of the head and the smaller ones at the corners of the mouth. The eyes are much larger in tilefish taken from the Gulf of Mexico.

Tilefish are excellent eating, but this large and valuable fish was not taken along the northern Atlantic Coast till 1879. Fishing for this species developed rapidly. Then, within three years, the tilefish nearly became extinct—probably because of the shift of a cold-water current into the narrow area they occupied. In March, 1882, steamships and fishing boats reported millions upon millions of dead tilefish floating at sea north of Delaware Bay. None was caught in the next few years. Gradually the fish returned, and after 1915 commercial fishing was taken up again. Peaks of 12 million pounds annually have been reached, but recent catches in North Atlantic waters have again been much smaller.

123

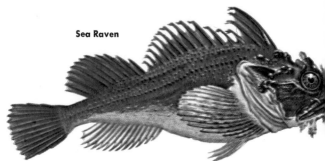

Sea Raven

SCULPINS are a family of odd, bizarre fishes with large, spiny or armored heads and short tapering bodies, sometimes soft, sometimes armored too. The pectoral fins, large and fanlike, are used by fresh-water species to hang onto stones. Sculpins are arctic or northern fishes found around the world in cooler waters. Most live on the bottom, feeding on crabs and small fishes. The flesh of Sculpins is edible, but because of their small size and unattractive form, sculpins are seldom eaten. They are a nuisance to fishermen. Eastern kinds are used for lobster bait.

LONGHORN SCULPIN has on its head sharp spines which make it hard to handle. Its color varies with the bottom on which it lives; usually it has light and dark blotches. Length to 1 ft.; weight to 1 lb. The Shorthorn Sculpin is similar, with smaller spines.

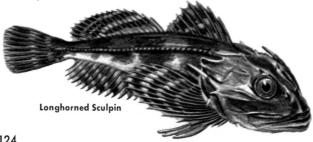

Longhorned Sculpin

Cabezon

SEA RAVEN (p. 124), a larger sculpin up to 20 in. long and weighing up to 5 lb., has large teeth and can bite severely when caught. The mottled skin is prickly. The Sea Raven swells up when caught. It prefers rocky bottoms in fairly deep water.

CABEZON is a large Pacific Sculpin, up to 30 in. long, weighing 20 to 25 lb. A favorite of anglers, it lives on hard or rocky bottoms in fairly shallow water. Good eating, but the roe is reported poisonous. Note soft skin, lack of scales, and large spine near eyes.

MOTTLED SCULPIN represents a small but widespread group of fresh-water sculpins. Some are lake dwellers, but the Mottled prefers streams with gravel bottoms in the Atlantic and eastern Mississippi drainage. Grows 4 to 6 in. long; is of no commercial value.

Mottled Sculpin

SEAROBINS and FLYING GURNARDS resemble sculpins, though each represents a different family.

Leopard Searobin has a large head and tapering body; mouth smaller than sculpin's, lower rays of pectoral fins free and modified for walking on the bottom. Found in the Gulf and Atlantic north to the Carolinas, this fish sometimes stirs up the bottom searching for crabs, worms, mollusks, and even small fishes. It grows to about 6 in. and forms part of the commercial "scrap" that is used in canned cat food.

Flying Gurnard is a southern Atlantic fish with enormous pectoral fins each divided into a larger and a smaller part. It takes leaps out of the water, but nothing like those of flyingfishes. The ventral fins are used as walking organs. The gill covers taper into thick spines. It grows to less than 1 ft. long.

Flying
Gurnard

Leopard
Searobin

Lumpfish

LUMPFISH and SEA SNAILS are odd creatures of northern waters found on both sides of the Atlantic. These interesting but unimportant fishes have unusual sucking discs, by which they cling to rocks and seaweeds.

Lumpfish is the larger (up to 20 in. and 20 lb.). It is a bottom dweller, found from the surf out to depths of 150 fathoms. Lumpfish often cling to lobster pots and feed on small invertebrates. They spawn in spring. The male guards the spongy masses of eggs.

Sea Snail

Sea Snails have an unusual tadpole shape. Small (under 6 in.) and soft-bodied, they are found as far south as New Jersey. All species have a well-developed sucking disc, formed from modified ventral fins. Sea Snails feed on small mollusks and other bottom invertebrates. They spawn early in spring.

Sea Snail: underside

127

Chilipepper

Bocaccio

ROCKFISHES are members of the scorpionfish family which give birth to young after they develop inside the female. About 60 species occur on our Pacific coast and a few on the Atlantic. All have armored heads like the related sculpins and searobins (pp. 124-126). More common in cool or temperate waters.

Bocaccio, found from British Columbia southward, grows up to 3 ft. long and weighs up to 20 lb. This very common and important food and game fish is olive brown with variable amounts of red, orange, and sometimes black.

Chilipepper is found along the California coast, more commonly to the south. It ranks with Bocaccio as the most important rockfish. Note the pink stripe along the lateral line. Length to 24 in.; weight to 10 lb.

OCEAN PERCH and SCORPIONFISH are eastern representatives of the rockfish family. Both are found along the Atlantic coast, and are temperate-water fishes.

Ocean Perch, sometimes called Redfish, grows to about 20 in. and weighs to 5 lb. It is very abundant and recently has become an important commercial species—more valuable than cod and a source of frozen filets and fish-sticks. It is taken by trawls in deep water, rarely caught by sport fishermen. Note the large eyes, gill openings, and the bright colors which fade rapidly after death. Like the Pacific Rockfish it gives birth to living young.

Plumed Scorpionfish is a more southerly scorpionfish representing a group of about 20 species on the Atlantic coast and a few on the Pacific. It lays eggs. To 8 in.

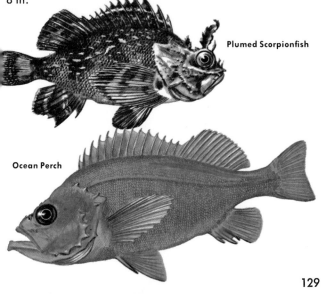

Plumed Scorpionfish

Ocean Perch

WRASSES are attractive, large-toothed, small-mouthed tropical fishes found in coral reefs and around rocks. They have a continuous dorsal fin. Additional grinding teeth in the throat aid in crushing mollusks. Scales are large and smooth. See Razorfish and Bluehead, p. 133.

HOGFISH, found north to the Carolinas but more common in Florida waters, is a fine food fish up to 2 ft. long. Note the three long spines in the dorsal fin and the bright colors, usually some shade of red, which changes rapidly.

TAUTOG, one of two northern wrasses, is found south to the Carolinas. A good food and game fish, 2 to 5 lb., it is found in summer around rocks, piers, and ledges, feeding on mussels and other mollusks. It winters in deeper waters.

CALIFORNIA SHEEPHEAD or California Redfish is a large wrasse of rocky shores from Monterey south. Male (left) and female are illustrated here. Dull red of female sometimes has dark blotches. A common sport fish. Length to 3 ft.; weight to 30 lb.

BUTTERFLYFISHES and ANGEL-FISHES form a group of compressed tropical reef dwellers of Florida waters with small mouths and teeth. Angelfishes differ from Butterflies in bearing a spine on the gill covers. Also, the dorsal fin of Angelfishes ends in a long filament.

QUEEN ANGELFISH is the largest of the group, growing to 2 ft. long. Like other angelfishes, it is good eating, though the group is not important as a food fish. Angelfishes feed on crabs, barnacles, and other invertebrates.

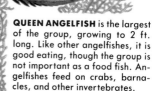

SPOTFIN BUTTERFLYFISH is a well-known reef dweller, marked by a dark line through the eye and another near the tail. This small fish (5 to 8 in.), fast and aggressive, feeds on small invertebrates.

FRENCH ANGELFISH (1 ft.) is a West Indies species as is the Gray Angelfish which occasionally spreads north to New Jersey. They are both popular salt-water aquarium fishes. Young have vertical yellow bands on a black background.

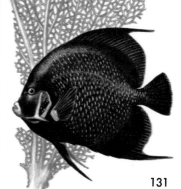

Rainbow
Parrotfish

TROPICAL MARINE FISHES form an important part of American sea life. Some are accidental stragglers; some come into our range during summer; some live the year round in Florida and Gulf waters. Southern California, with cooler waters, has fewer tropical species.

SERGEANT MAJOR, named for its stripes, and Reef Fish, common on coral reefs, are in the damselfish family. Range north to Florida. Males guard eggs. 6 in.

RAINBOW PARROTFISH is one of the largest herbivorous and coral-eating reef dwellers. It grows up to 3 ft. The Parrotfish family includes brightly colored species, with fused, nipping teeth that can cut a hook in two.

SPADEFISH, a relative of angelfishes (p. 131), is larger (to 3 ft.) and a fine food and game fish. A favorite target of skin divers. There is also a Pacific Spadefish.

Spadefish

Sergeant Major

Stoplight Parrotfish

**Bluehead
(a Wrasse)**

**Pearly Razor Fish
(a Wrasse)**

Reef Fish

Ocean Triggerfish

Gray Triggerfish

TRIGGERFISHES are so named because the first of the three stout spines of the dorsal fin is locked upright by the second when the fish is disturbed. It will drop only when the second spine is pressed as a trigger. Triggerfishes are compressed fishes almost as high as long, with heavy scales and tough skin. Ventral fins are much reduced or absent. These fishes average about 1 ft., rarely weighing over 1 lb. All are tropical, from Florida and the West Indies.

Gray Triggerfish is variably colored, usually a mottled brown, yellow, or gray. Length, about 1 ft. It gets farther north than other species. Ocean Triggerfish is larger, up to 2 ft., and weighs 3 to 5 lb. or more.

DORSAL FIN TRIGGER MECHANISM

fin up

fin released

fin down

Orange Filefish

Planehead Filefish

FILEFISHES have tiny, hard scales set in a tough skin which was once used as sandpaper—hence their name. They are relatives of triggerfishes, but have only one dorsal spine instead of three. The ventral fins are reduced or absent. Filefishes are common in northern and temperate waters, though the family is a tropical one. They feed on algae and small invertebrates.

Planehead Filefish rarely gets over 10 in. long. It is found north to Cape Cod but is more common in the south. The Fringed Filefish, of southern waters, is similar but has a larger ventral flap than the Planehead Filefish.

Orange Filefish, a longer, less deep species, may reach a length of 2 ft. This one is more common in the Gulf of Mexico and along the Florida coast. The Orange Filefish is not always orange, but is mottled, with olive gray, orange, or white.

TRUNKFISHES are marine oddities. The body scales fuse, forming a solid, triangular shell from which the moving fins and tail protrude. The boxlike shell is made up of six-sided plates, each firmly attached to those which surround it. The Trunkfishes are therefore slow and limited in their movements. When they are found north of their southern range they have usually been carried along by the Gulf Stream. The young are more rounded and, in some species, are brightly colored.

Common Trunkfish is found mainly in Florida waters but also to the north as far as Cape Cod. Only very small fish are found that far north. Up to 10 in.

Scrawled Cowfish is a larger trunkfish, sometimes over a foot long. Like other trunkfishes it is edible. Trunkfishes are sometimes baked in their own shells.

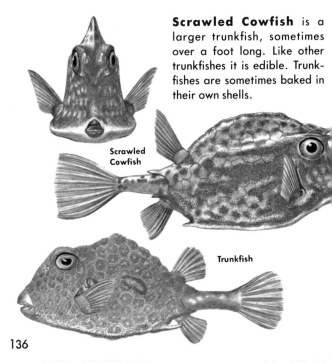

Scrawled
Cowfish

Trunkfish

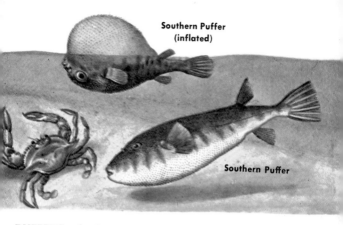

Southern Puffer
(inflated)

Southern Puffer

PUFFERS, also known as Swellfishes, can quickly inflate their bodies with air or water till they swell to three times normal size. When danger is past, they deflate just as rapidly. Puffers are found all along the Atlantic Coast and at points along the Pacific Coast. They live in shallow water, feeding on crabs and other invertebrates. Some puffers are poisonous. Since the poison is extremely potent, it is unwise to use puffers as food.

Smooth Puffer, one of the largest species, is most common in southern waters. It has prickles confined to area on belly. Up to 2 ft.

Northern Puffer is not common north of Cape Cod. It spawns in summer. Bandtail Puffer, from Florida south, and Southern Puffer of the Gulf, are similar in form and size.

Smooth Puffer

137

Porcupinefish

PORCUPINEFISH and BURRFISH are closely related to the puffers, but in addition to their ability to swell, their skin is covered with stout spines which make them dangerous to other fishes and hard to handle. These are tropical fishes, occasionally found north to Cape Cod, usually in shallow water, where they feed on small invertebrates. Of no commercial value, but interesting because of their form, members of this family and the puffers are found in the Pacific south of our border.

Porcupinefish has long, stout spines which stick out in all directions. Length, 1 ft.; occasionally 3 ft.

Striped Burrfish or Spiny Boxfish is a common species with short, stout spines. It is so slow it provides sport for skin divers, who can easily catch them. 10 in.

Striped Burrfish

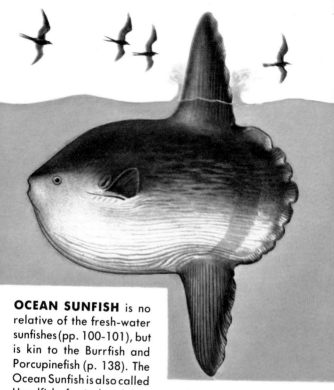

OCEAN SUNFISH is no relative of the fresh-water sunfishes (pp. 100-101), but is kin to the Burrfish and Porcupinefish (p. 138). The Ocean Sunfish is also called Headfish, for its head dominates the entire body. It prefers warmer waters, though it occurs widely in all seas. This odd, lazy fish is one of three species in our waters. Specimens 6 ft. long and 600 lb. have been caught; the record weight is about a ton. Food is small marine invertebrates. The Ocean Sunfish has a leathery outer skin with a thick tough white layer beneath. Its bones are soft and weak, and its movements are limited. Harpooned as a game fish, it has no use as food.

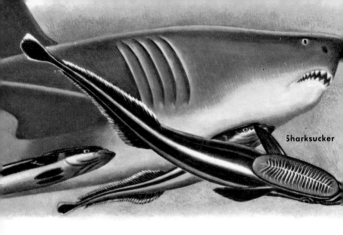

Sharksucker

REMORAS are also called Sharksuckers because of the unusual, oval sucking disc on the top of the head. With this they attach themselves to swordfish, sharks, or any other large fish for a free ride. Remoras are not parasites, nor do they "guide" their host. They merely share left-over dinner scraps. The sucking disc developed from the front dorsal fin; muscular flaps open to create the suction. There are several species of remora. They all prefer warmer waters. The Sharksucker, illustrated above, is the largest and most common, usually about 2 ft. long, sometimes a foot longer. Remoras are found on other fishes such as Drums, Swordfish, and Marlins; sometimes on large sea turtles. They commonly attach to skin divers.

Northern Stargazer

STARGAZERS are southern fishes best known from Atlantic species, which are seldom over 1 ft. long. Mouth, nostrils, and eyes high in the head make it possible for Stargazers to lie buried in the sand awaiting unwary crustaceans. Some Stargazers have, in the top

electric organs on head of Stargazer

of their heads, electrical cells which have developed from the optic nerve. These can give a strong shock to an animal or person. When the mouth opens to grasp an animal, an accompanying shock paralyzes the prey.

Gulf Toadfish

Atlantic Midshipman

TOADFISH, found on muddy bottoms of shallow water, feed on crustaceans, mollusks, and small fishes. Length, to 1 ft. The male guards the eggs, which may rest in an old shell or even in a tin can or bottle. He bites viciously while on duty. Midshipman (see also p. 51), of toadfish family, lays and guards eggs in much the same manner.

Toadfish guarding eggs

male

Kelp Greenling

female

GREENLINGS are a Pacific family most abundant in waters north of Monterey. Several species, more or less common, which grow to about 20 in. long, are all desirable game fish. They are taken close to shore in all seasons but never appear in large enough numbers to be important in commercial fisheries. Greenlings are characterized by one or two pairs of small fleshy flaps on the top of the head. The Kelp Greenling, illustrated above, is sometimes called Seatrout or Rockfish, though both these names are misleading. The male and female differ in color and form of markings—an uncommon occurrence among fishes. Rock Greenlings, or Red Rock Trout, are usually brown (some are green); they are northern fishes. The White-spotted Greenling is more common in Oregon waters and northward.

KELPFISHES represent another Pacific family. Most species are found all along the coast near rocky shores and in kelp beds. Most are small fishes (4 to 8 in. long) which have little economic importance and even lack common names. The kelpfishes are related to the blennies (pp. 144-145).

Giant Kelpfish, the species illustrated above and below, is much larger than its relatives—18 to 24 in. long. It is often caught by anglers and finds its way into commercial nets. It illustrates the protective coloration seen so often in fishes. Those living in kelp beds, above, are reddish and mottled, so they blend with the swaying kelps. Those living in eelgrass, below, are silver and green, matching those surroundings. This kelpfish is edible, though the flesh may have the same green color as the skin.

BLENNIES and GOBIES are two large families of small fishes, difficult to identify, yet seen by practically everyone who has walked along the beaches. These are the fishes of tide pools, oyster beds, and mud flats. They live in eelgrass and in the shallows and inlets. Some prefer brackish or even fresh water. None is of special economic importance, yet all are of value as part of the neverending cycle of marine life.

BLENNIES include a group of tropical species and another group of arctic species. The northern ones are larger. Some blennies are scaled; others have naked skins. Some have fleshy filaments or fringes on their heads. The ventral fins are reduced to one spine and a few soft rays. They eat any small animals.

GOBIES also abound in shallow water, especially along southern shores. They are both scaled and naked, and all have ventral fins closely joined or modified to form a sucking disc, as in their relatives, the clingfishes.

STRIPED BLENNY occurs as far north as New York in shallow water. Lays eggs in empty shells and rock crevices. Up to 5 in.

FRECKLED BLENNY is found close to shore from the Carolinas all around the Gulf to Texas. Common in tide pools. Up to 3 in.

NAKED GOBY is a scaleless species found from Cape Cod south. Common in southern bays, inlets; often in empty shells. Up to 3 in.

SHARPTAIL GOBY lives in brackish or salt water in bays along the Gulf Coast. Length, about 6 in.— sometimes up to 10 in.

FAT SLEEPER, related to the Gobies, thrives in fresh, salt, or brackish water. Occasionally large enough to be a food fish.

LONGJAW MUDSUCKER, a Pacific Goby, is much in demand as a bait fish. Very hardy. Length, 3 to 4 in.; rarely larger.

145

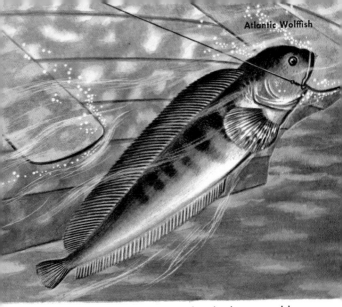

WOLFFISHES represent a family that resembles over-grown blennies with large, tusk-like teeth. All are northern fishes, with a preference for arctic waters on both sides of the Atlantic. Wolffishes have a single, long dorsal fin, like blennies, but the tips of the spines are soft. Two species occur north of Cape Cod, one off Nova Scotia, and one along our Pacific Coast.

Atlantic Wolffish is marked by about a dozen dark vertical bars along its sides. Found from the shoreline out to depths of 500 or 600 ft., it is a solitary fish, feeding on sea urchins, mollusks, and crustaceans. It is often caught in cod nets and is sometimes taken on lines. It is a vicious fish and can bite dangerously. Length, to 6 ft.; average is less than 3. Weight, to 40 lb. Good eating; it is caught commercially in quantity and often sold as "ocean catfish."

146

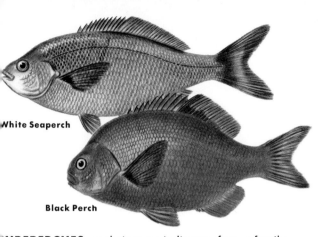

White Seaperch

Black Perch

SURFPERCHES, as their name indicates, form a family of perch-like fishes, many living in the surf, found all along the Pacific Coast. Some prefer deeper water; and there is a single fresh-water species. Surfperches bear their young alive. Adults are small, compressed fishes, usually less than 1 ft. long and weighing not much over 1 lb. Often caught by sportsmen, they also form a minor part of the commercial haul. The three species illustrated on this page are representative of the family, and are among the best known and most common.

Barred Surfperch

Sargassumfish

SARGASSUMFISH are small anglers which live in the floating sargassum beds of the warmer Atlantic. Their color and adaptations, such as the armlike pectoral fins, enable them to thrive in this limited environment. These fish grow to about 6 in., with large mouths and deep bodies. They feed on other fishes often as large as they. Sargassumfish sometimes drift north in patches of weeds and are found past Cape Cod. Their gill openings are two small openings, located behind the pectoral fins.

WARTED SEADEVIL is a deep-sea angler found 200 to 600 fathoms down, or more. Note the luminous "bait" which dangles in front of the mouth. Males are parasitic, attaching themselves to the females and growing fast to them, their eyes and digestive organs ceasing to develop. Several species; 6 to 40 in. long.

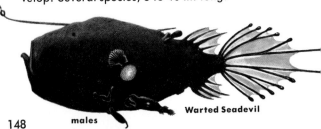

males

Warted Seadevil

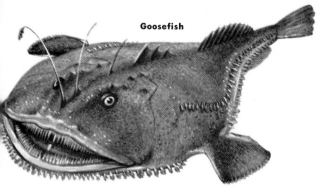

Goosefish

GOOSEFISH is the biggest angler and is odd in many other ways. It has a small gill opening behind armlike pectoral fins like the Sargassumfish and Batfish. Its first dorsal spine has become a long rod, at the end of which it dangles a "bait" with which it has been observed to attract other fishes by flashing it back and forth like a worm before its vast mouth; it opens its mouth, then sucks its prey down into its gullet. The goosefish can swallow a fish almost as big as itself and sometimes does; one specimen contained seven ducks. Goosefish grow 2 to 4 ft. long and weigh up to 50 lb.

SHORTNOSE BATFISH, another angler, like the goosefish has pectoral fins at the end of a bony joint. Batfish are small (8 to 12 in.), and are found in warm waters.

top view

Shortnose Batfish

149

RED DORY grades from pink to silvery. Fins yellowish, except black and white ventrals. 600 to 1,200 ft. deep.

DEEP-SEA FISHES is a term often applied to species living below the 100 fathom (600 ft.) level. Here, many fishes and marine invertebrates are colored a bright red. The silvery colors and showy markings of shallow-water fishes are usually lacking. Below 200 fathoms more fishes tend to be black or dark brown in color and possess luminous organs (see p. 51). Some have large mouths and expandable stomachs and can swallow fishes larger than themselves. Other deep-sea fishes have a long tentacle ending in a "bait" that dangles before their mouth and attracts their prey.

The deep-sea bottom may be covered with forests of sponges, crinoids and other invertebrates which provide food for fishes. Deeper bottoms may be soft mud and fishes living there may have fins ending in long filaments to support them above the soft ooze that covers mile after mile of ocean floor. Less is known of the life histories of the fishes living here.

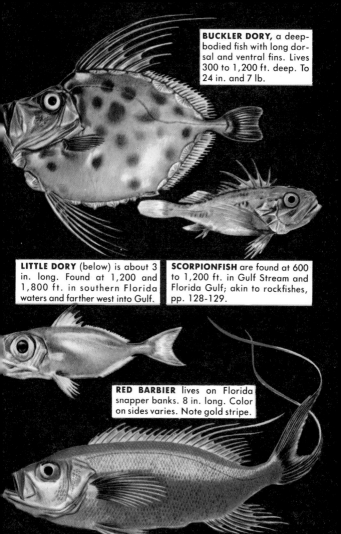

BUCKLER DORY, a deep-bodied fish with long dorsal and ventral fins. Lives 300 to 1,200 ft. deep. To 24 in. and 7 lb.

LITTLE DORY (below) is about 3 in. long. Found at 1,200 and 1,800 ft. in southern Florida waters and farther west into Gulf.

SCORPIONFISH are found at 600 to 1,200 ft. in Gulf Stream and Florida Gulf; akin to rockfishes, pp. 128-129.

RED BARBIER lives on Florida snapper banks. 8 in. long. Color on sides varies. Note gold stripe.

Dolphin

Blackfish

ANIMALS MISTAKEN FOR FISHES

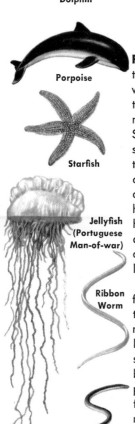
Porpoise

Starfish

Jellyfish (Portuguese Man-of-war)

Ribbon Worm

Sea Snake

FISHES make up only a small fraction of the animal life of the sea, which ranges from microscopic protozoa to whales. Many forms of marine life are obviously not fishes. Some others are fishlike and are a source of confusion. Foremost of these are the marine mammals: the dolphins, porpoises, blackfishes, and whales. Whales and their kin have horizontal flukes, while fishes have vertical tails. The mammals are warm-blooded air breathers and must come up for air sooner or later.

Other animals confused with fishes are not fishlike but often have the word "fish" as part of their name. The starfish has no backbone like fishes, but has stiff arms and a spiny, limy skin. Jellyfishes lack a backbone also and are much simpler than fishes. Sea Snakes are not fishes, nor are the free-swimming marine worms and other ocean animals without backbones. For more about them read SEASHORES (p. 153).

BOOKS TO READ

FISHES are perhaps more difficult to identify than other backboned animals. Accurate identification depends on a careful study of the fishes, with attention to the structure of the fins, teeth, kind of scales, and number of rows of them.

Listed below is a group of books to enrich your reading about fishes. Most are non-technical; the rest are nearly so.

Breder, Charles M. Jr., FIELD BOOK OF MARINE FISHES OF THE ATLANTIC COAST, G. P. Putnam's Sons, New York, 1948. A complete but necessarily brief guide to Atlantic species. Photographs and drawings.

Curtis, Brian, THE LIFE STORY OF THE FISH, Harcourt, Brace, and Co., New York, 1949. A very readable, informal biology of fishes—what they are, how they live, breathe, swim, and see. Adds another dimension to fish identification.

Hubbs and Lagler, FISHES OF THE GREAT LAKES REGION, Cranbrook Institute of Science, Bloomfield Hills, Mich., 1947. A systematic regional guide.

LaMonte, Francesca, NORTH AMERICAN GAME FISHES, Doubleday and Co., New York, 1945. A concise guide to fresh- and salt-water game fishes with some fine colored plates and a table of record weights.

Roedel, Phil M., COMMON OCEAN FISHES OF THE CALIFORNIA COAST, State of Calif. Dept. of Fish and Game, Sacramento, Calif., 1953. (Fish Bulletin No. 91). An excellent guide. Direct, informative text and fine photographic illustrations.

Smith, Philip W., THE FISHES OF ILLINOIS, published for the Ill. State Nat. Hist. Survey by the Univ. of Ill. Press, Urbana, Chicago, London, 1979. Excellent for fresh-water fish identification and ecology.

Zim and Ingle, SEASHORES, A Golden Guide, Golden Press, New York, 1955. A beginner's guide to all marine life of the shores except fishes, hence a helpful supplement. Full-color illustrations.

(ventral view)

CLING FISH, a 4-in. relative of blennies.

Study fishes in detail at every opportunity. If you are a good swimmer, try skin diving. Visit aquaria and museums to see living specimens and prepared exhibits.

Shedd Aquarium, Chicago, Ill.
Marine Studios, Marineland, Fla.
Steinhart Aquarium, San Francisco, Calif.
John Pennekamp Coral Reef State Park, Key Largo, Fla.
Municipal Aquarium, Key West, Fla.
American Museum of Natural History, New York City
Chicago Natural History Museum, Chicago, Ill.

Marine biological stations operate in connection with universities and government conservation departments. Research facilities and courses may be available. Inquire before visiting.

Univ. of Mich. Biol. Station, Douglas Lake, Cheboygan, Mich.
Univ. of Okla. Biol. Station, Lake Texoma, Willis, Okla.
Univ. of Minn. Lake Itaska Biol. Station, Lake Itaska P.O., Minn.
Franz Stone Inst. of Hydrobiology, Put-in-Bay, Ohio
Marine Biological Laboratory, Woods Hole, Mass.
Duke Univ. Marine Laboratory, Beaufort, N.C.
Univ. of Miami Marine Laboratory, Coral Gables, Fla.
Gulf Coast Research Laboratory, Ocean Springs, Miss.
Institute of Marine Science, Port Aransas, Tex.
Scripps Institute of Oceanography, La Jolla, Calif.
Friday Harbor Laboratories, Univ. of Wash., Friday Harbor, Wash.

SCIENTIFIC NAMES

The following pages list the scientific names of the species illustrated. The number refers to the pages on which the fish is pictured; then follows a name or part of a name that distinguishes the fish from others on that page; then the scientific name—first the genus, then the species. If the genus name is abbreviated, it is the same as the one just above it. Atlantic, Pacific, and fresh-water species are identified by A, P, and F.

1 Trichiurus lepturus, A
2 Trout: Salmo aguabonita, F
Triggerfish: Balistes vetula, A
8 Morone saxatilis, APF

19 Lamprey: Petromyzon marinus, AF
Trout: Salvelinus namaycush, F
Hagfish: Myxine glutinosa, A

22 Hammer: Sphyrna zygaena, AP
Sandbar: Carcharhinus plumbeus, A
Dogfish: Squalus acanthias, AP
Nurse: Ginglymostoma cirratum, A
23 White: Carcharadon carcharias, AP
Tiger: Galeocerdo cuvieri, AP
Thresher: Alopias vulpinus, AP
Soupfin: Galeorhinus zyopterus, P
24 Rhincodon typus, AP
25 Manta birostris, A
26 Barndoor: Raja laevis, A
Little Skate: R. erinacea, A
Torpedo: Torpedo nobiliana, A
27 Bluntnose: Dasyatis sayi, A
Round: Urolophus halleri, P
Butterfly: Gymnura micrura, A
28 Sawfish: Pristis pectinata, A
Guitarfish: Rhinobatos lentiginosus, A
29 Ratfish: Hydrolagus colliei, P
Chimaera: Chimaera affinis, A
32 Atl. Sturgeon: Acipenser oxyrhynchus, AF
Shovelnose St.: Scaphirhynchus platorhynchus spathula, F
Paddlefish: Polyodon spathula, F
33 Longnose: Lepisosteus osseus, F
Shortnose: L. platostomus, F
34 Elops saurus, A
35 Tarpon: Megalops atlantica, A
Bonefish: Albula vulpes, A
36 Alosa pseudoharengus, AF
37 A. sapidissima, APF
38 Sardinops sagax, P
39 Brevoortia tyrannus, A
40 Herring: Clupea harengus, A
Shad: Dorosoma cepedianum, AF
41 Bay: Anchoa mitchilli, AF
Northern: Engraulis mordax, P
42 Chum: Oncorhynchus keta, PF
Pink: O. gorbuscha, APF
43 Chinook: O. tshawytscha, PF
Coho: O. kisutch, APF
44 O. nerka, PF
45 Sebago, Atlantic: Salmo salar, AF
Cutthroat: S. clarki, PF
47 Brook: Salvelinus fontinalis, AF
Rainbow: Salmo gairdneri, AF
Dolly: Salvelinus malma, PF
Lake Tr.: S. namaycush, F

48 Lake Wh.: Coregonus clupeaformis, AF
Shortjaw: C. zenithicus, F
49 Cisco: C. artedii, F
Round Wh.: Prosopium cylindraceum, F
Grayling: Thymallus arcticus, F
50 Rainbow: Osmerus mordax, APF
Whitebait: Allosmerus elongatus, P
51 Hatchet: Sternoptyx diaphana, A
Lantern: Myctophum affine, A
52 Anguilla rostrata, AF
53 Conger: Conger oceanicus, A
Worm: Myrophis punctatus, A
54 Green: Gymnothorax funebris, A
Spotted: G. moringa, A
55 Smallmouth: Ictiobus bubalis, F
Bigm: I. cyrpinellus, F
56 White: Catostomus commersoni, F
Hog: Hypentelium nigricans, F
Quillback: Carpiodes cyprinus, F
Redhorse: Moxostoma macrolepidotum, F
57 Cyprinus carpio, F
58 Dace: Clinostomus elongatus, F
Creek Ch.: Semotilus atromaculatus, F
Golden Sh.: Notemigonus crysoleucas, F
59 Thicktail Chub: Gila crassicauda, F
Dace: Phoxinus erythrogaster, F
Emerald Sh.: Notropis atherinoides, F
Cutlips: Exoglossum maxillingua, F
60 Ictalurus punctatus, F
61 Tom: Noturus miurus, F
Stonecat: N. flavus, F
Flathead: Pylodictis olivaris, F
Blue: Ictalurus furcatus, F
62 Black: I. melas, F
Yellow: I. natalis, F
Brown: I. nebulosus, F
63 Gafftopsail: Bagre marinus, A
Hardhead: Arias felis, A
65 Pike: Esox lucius, F
Muskell: E. masquinongy, F
Grass: E. americanus, F
Chain: E. niger, F
66 Banded: Fundulus diaphanus, F
Sheepshead: Cyprinodon variegatus, AF
Mosquitofish: Gambusia affinis, AF
Mummichog: Fundulus heteroclitus, AF

67 Needle: Strongylura marina, A
Halfbeak: Hyporhamphus unifas-
ciatus, AP
Ballyhoo: Hemiramphus brasiliensis, A
68 Cypselurus melanurus, A
69 Blackwing: Hirundichthys rondeleti, AP
California: Cypselurus californicus, P
Margined: C. cyanopterus, A
70 Lota lota, F
71 Gadus morhua, A
72 Tomcod: Microgadus tomcod, AF
Pollock: Pollachius virens, A
73 Melanogrammus aeglefinns, A
74 Merluccius bilinearis, A
75 White: Urophycis tenuis, A
Red: U. chuss, A
Southern: U. floridana, A
76 Trinectes maculatus, A
77 Smooth: Liopsetta putnami, A
Plaice: Hippoglossoides plates-
soides, A
South. Flounder: Paralichthys
lethostigma, A
78 Cal. Halibut: Paralichthys californicus, P
Starry Fl.: Platichthys stellatus, PF
Atl. Hal.: Hippoglossus hippoglossus, A
79 Brook: Culaea inconstans, F
Threespine: Gasterosteus aculea-
tus, APF
80 Seahorse: Hippocampus erectus, A
Pipefish: Syngnathus fuscus, A
81 Mullet: Mugil cephalus, AP
Inland: Menidia beryllina, AF
Brook: Labidesthes sicculus, F
82 Grunion: Leuresthes tenuis, P
Jacksmelt: Atherinopsis califor-
niensis, P
83 Pac.: Sphyraena argentea, P
Great: S. barracuda, A
84 Atl.: Scomber scombrus, A
Chub: S. japonicus, AP
Spanish: Scomberomorus maculatus, A
85 King: S. cavalla, A
Wahoo: Acanthocybium solan-
deri, A
86 Little Tunny: Euthynnus alletera-
tus, A
Skipjack: E. pelamis, AP
Albacore: Thunnus alalunga, AP
Bonito: Sarda sarda, A
87 Bluefin: Thunnus thynnus, AP
Yellowfin: Thunnus albacores, AP

88 Blue: Makaira nigricans, AP
Striped: Tetrapturus audax, P
White: T. albidus, A
89 Istiophorus platypterus, AP
90 Swordfish: Xiphias gladius, AP
Lizardfish: Synodus foetens, A
91 Coryphaena hippurus, AP
92 Butter: Poronotus triacanthus,
A
Harvest: Peprilus alepidotus, A
93 Moonfish: Selene setapinnis, A
Lookdown: S. vomer, A
94 Crevalle: Caranx hippos, A
Amberjack: Seriola dumerili, A
95 Jack: Trachurus symmetricus, P
Yellowtail: Seriola lalandei, P
Florida Pompano: Trachinotus
carolinus, A
Permit: T. falcatus, A
96 Pilotfish: Naucrates ductor, AP
Bluefish: Pomatomus saltatrix, A
97 Perch: Perca flavescens, F
Walleye: Stizostedion vitreum, F
Rainbow: Etheostoma caeru-
leum, F
Johnny: E. nigrum, F
98 Archoplites interruptus, F
99 Largemouth: Micropterus sal-
moides, F
Smallmouth: M. dolomieui, F
Spotted: M. punctulatus, F
100 Lepomis macrochirus, F
101 Pumpkinseed: L. gibbosus, F
Green: L. cyanellus, F
Longear: L. megalotis, F
102 L. microlophus, F
103 Spotted: L. punctatus, F
Warmouth: Chaenobryttus gulosus, F
Bass: Ambloplites rupestris, F
104 Black: Pomoxis nigromaculatus, F
White: P. annularis, F
106 Giant: Stereolepis gigas, P
White: Morone chrysops, F
107 Wh. Perch: M. americana, AF
Yel. Bass: M. mississippiensis, F
108 Black: Centropristis striata, A
Kelp: Paralabrax clathratus, P
109 Warsaw: Epinephelus nigritus, A
Jewfish: E. itajara, A
110 Yellowfin: Mycteroperca vene-
nosa, A
Red: Epinephelus morio, A
Black: Mycteroperca bonaci, A
111 Snook: Centropomus undecimalis, A
Tripletail: Lobotes surinamensis, A

112 Lutjanus apodus, A
113 Red: L. campechanus, A
Gray: L. griseus, AF
Yellow: Ocyurus chrysurus, A
114 Anisotremus virginicus, A
115 White: Haemulon plumieri, A
Bluestriped: H. sciurus, A
Tomtate: H. aurolineatum, A
Pigfish: Orthopristis chrysoptera, AF
116 Scup: Stenotomus chrysops, A
Sheepshead: Archosargus probatocephalus, A
117 Jolt: Calamus bajonado, A
Pin: Lagodon rhomboides, AF
Opaleye: Girella nigricans, P
118 Chub: Kyphosus sectatrix, A
Silver Jenny: Eucinostomus gula, A
119 Weakfish: Cynoscion regalis, A
Spotted: C. nebulosus, AF
Bass: Atractoscion nobilis, P
120 Atl.: Micropogonias undulatus, A
Spotfin: Roncador stearnsi, P
121 Red: Sciaenops ocellatus, AF
Black: Pogonias cromis, A
122 So. King: Menticirrhus americanus, A
Corbina: M. undulatus, P
123 Lopholatilus chamaeleonticeps, A
124 Sea Raven: Hemitripterus americanus, A
Sculpin: Myoxocephalus octodecemspinosus, A
125 Cabezon: Scorpaenichthys marmoratus, P
Sculpin: Cottus bairdi, F
126 Robin: Prionotus scitulus, A
Gurnard: Dactylopterus volitans, A
127 Lump: Cyclopterus lumpus, A
Snail: Liparis atlanticus, A
128 Chili: Sebastes goodei, P
Bocaccio: S. paucispinis, P
129 Plumed: Scorpaena grandicornis, A
Ocean P.: Sebastes marinus, A
130 Hogfish: Lachnolaimus maximus, A
Tautog: Tautoga onitis, A
Sheephead: Semicossyphus pulcher, A
131 Queen: Holacanthus ciliaris, A
Spotfin: Chaetodon ocellatus, A
French: Pomacanthus paru, A

132 Parrot: Scarus guacamaia, A
Spade: Chaetodipterus faber, A
Sgt.: Abudefduf saxatilis, A
133 Stoplight: Sparisoma viride, A
Bluehead: Thalassoma bifasciatum, A
Razor: Hemipteronotus novacula, A
Reef: Chromis marginatus, A
134 Ocean: Canthidermis sufflamen, A
Gray: Balistes capriscus, A
135 Orange: Aluterus schoepfi, A
Planehead: Monacanthus hispidus, A
136 Cowfish: Lactophrys quadricornis, A
Trunkfish: L. trigonus, A
137 Southern: Sphoeroides nephelus, A
Smooth: Lagocephalus laevigatus, A
138 Porcupine: Diodon hystrix, AP
Burr: Chilomycterus schoepfi, A
139 Mola mola, AP
140 Sharksucker: Echeneis naucrates, A
Stargazer: Astroscopus guttatus, A
141 Midshipman: Porichthys plectrodon, A
Toadfish: Opsanus beta, A
142 Hexagrammos decagrammus, P
143 Heterostichus rostratus, P
144 Striped: Chasmodes bosquianus, A
Freckled: Hypsoblennius ionthas, A
145 Naked: Gobiosoma bosci, AF
Sharptail: Gobionellus hastatus, A
Sleeper: Dormitator maculatus, A
Long: Gillichthys mirabilis, P
146 Anarhichas lupus, A
147 White: Phanerodon furcatus, A
Black: Embiotoca jacksoni, P
Barred: Amphistichus argenteus, P
148 Sargassum: Histrio histrio, A
Seadevil: Cryptopsaras couesi, A
149 Goose: Lophius americanus, A
Bat: Ogcocephalus nasutus, A
150 Zenion roseus, A
151 Buckler: Zenopsis conchifera, A
Little: Zenion hololepis, A
Scorp.: Setarches parmatus, A
Barbier: Hemanthias vivanus, A

157

INDEX

Asterisks (*) designate pages where fishes are pictured. Keep in mind that in th[is] index both preferred and alternate names are listed, but the pictures ar[e] captioned with the preferred names only.

MEASURING SCALE (IN MILLIMETERS AND CENTIMETERS)

MEASURING SCALE (IN INCHES)